*The Politics
of
Public Management*

The Politics
of
Public Management

Philip B. Heymann

NEW HAVEN AND LONDON, YALE UNIVERSITY PRESS

Designed by Christopher Harris
and set in Times Roman type by
The Composing Room of Michigan, Inc.
Printed in the United States of America by
Vail-Ballou Press, Binghamton, N.Y.

The paper in this book meets the guidelines for
permanence and durability of the Committee on
Production Guidelines for Book Longevity of the
Council on Library Resources.

Library of Congress Cataloging-in-Publication Data

Heymann, Philip B.
   The politics of public management.

   Includes index.
   1. United States—Politics and government—Decision
making.   2. Public administration.   I. Title.
JK261.H49   1987   353'.07'25   86-40577
ISBN 0–300–03777–5 (alk. paper)

10   9   8   7   6   5   4   3   2   1

To Ann,
   My Frequent Editor,
   My Constant Supporter,
   and
   My Dearest Friend

Contents

Preface / ix

Part I The Politics of Management

1. *The World of the Public Manager* / 3
2. *Strategy for a Government Organization* / 12
3. *Strategy and Leadership* / 25
4. *Ends and Means* / 42
5. *Departmental Strategy and Presidential Stakes* / 5(
6. *Sources of Legitimacy* / 74
7. *Strategic Relations among Organizations Sharing a Common Responsibility* / 90

Part II The Management of Politics

8. *A Closer Look at the Hill* / 109
9. *Legislative Tactics* / 125
10. *The Meaning of "Resources" in a Political Setting* / 145
11. *Reshaping the Political Environment* / 164
    Appendix: Kennedy School Case Studies / 190
    Index / 191

Preface

In March 1966 I was appointed acting administrator of the Bureau of Security and Consular Affairs (SCA), a State Department unit that began as the creation of the fiercely anticommunist senators and congressmen of the 1950s but had taken on a decidedly liberal coloration in the early 1960s under the Kennedy administration. My predecessor and former boss, Abba Schwartz, had resigned shortly after my arrival amid a flurry of front-page newspaper articles noting that there had been a secret reorganization plan designed to push him aside and defining his resignation as a victory of the hardliners over the liberals, a victory that would have been impossible, many papers suggested, if John F. Kennedy were still president.

Two years in the Air Force's Office of Special Investigations and four years in the Department of Justice had hardly prepared me for the intensely political world of SCA. The bureau was established in 1952 to supervise action on the requests of foreigners for visas (the permission one government grants to the citizens of another to enter the former's territory) and on the requests of U.S. citizens for passports permitting them to travel abroad. Considerations of internal security were prominent throughout the 1950s in the Visa Office and the Passport Office, both of which reported to the administrator of SCA. The bureau originally also had charge of guaranteeing the internal security of the Department of State and the loyalty of its personnel, but these responsibilities had been divested before my arrival.

When I arrived the Passport Office was still headed by Frances Knight, a powerful bureaucratic and congressional infighter. She had been appointed in 1955 to replace Ruth Shipley, who was even more passionately anticommunist than Ms. Knight, though hardly as competent in either administration or politics. Over the years Ms. Knight consolidated her power, while supervisors at higher levels came and went. She carefully built a constituency among powerful conservatives in both houses of the Congress. Special consideration and assistance in the delivery of passports made her widely popular on Capitol hill.

The conservatives who had been dominant in the State Department and on the hill during the 1950s encountered some strong opposition in the early 1960s. For Knight the opposition was symbolized by Abba Schwartz, who was determined to move our travel policies toward greater openness. In particular, the two battled over the right of a person denied a passport on the ground of being communist to confront his or her accusers.* Schwartz won, but these battles escalated into a bitter war in which differences in personality heightened the conflict of ideologies. Knight used her powers of influence on the hill to have Schwartz harassed constantly. He retaliated with his powers in the bureau. All this was the background to a secret effort to reorganize the bureau out of existence, leading to Schwartz's resignation.

My objectives when I was appointed acting administrator were simple enough. I wanted to continue Schwartz's liberal, free-travel policies; to bring some peace to that area of constant conflict; to develop a personal reputation for competence in managing a government agency; and to improve the atmosphere for a variety of initiatives promoting a more open society. With the first objective in mind, I made what seemed a rather straightforward decision within a few weeks of assuming the position. Seeing a cable signed by Frances Knight asking one of our embassies for all information that came to its attention on a traveling American, I directed her personally and in writing to keep the Passport Office out of the investigative business unless some investigative agency had requested help. We were, I said perhaps too piously, not charged by Congress with any investigative responsibilities. I could find no sign in the file of a request from the FBI, although weeks later Knight produced one.

I still regale students with the account of what ensued in the next two or

---

*In the following chapters, the pronoun "he" will generally, though not always, be used to stand for both sexes. Though I regret the sacrifice of apparent gender neutrality, the practice allows me to avoid frequent use of the cumbersome "he or she" or a frequent confusing rotation of terms.

three weeks. The results were a shambles. Within a month of taking over I had completely lost control of the situation. Knight's cable and my directive to her were promptly leaked to the press. I abruptly found myself engaged in a front-page battle with her that drew in, as allies or opponents, powerful senators, the secretary of state, and the attorney general. In this whirlwind of impassioned confusion, the director of the FBI, J. Edgar Hoover, decided I was a new political opponent. He wrote to the secretary of state suggesting my dismissal and then temporarily abandoned a not very useful and not very offensive investigative program under which the FBI requested information on Americans abroad.

But I did not accomplish any of my broader objectives. I would find it harder, not easier, to pursue my agenda in a political context so recently riven by a meaningless conflict between liberals and conservatives. No prospect remained of bringing some peace and reason to the area. Having failed to show much competence in managing one troubled area, I would find it harder to convince others to allow me to handle necessary decisions in the future. I decided then and there that I had better study what had gone wrong.

By a year later I had learned some things essential to doing better. Before leaving the Bureau of Security and Consular Affairs I wanted to encourage the travel of foreigners to the United States by extending the duration of visas allowing brief visits to the United States. Under existing rules visas had to be renewed every four years. I saw no reason why some visas could not remain valid until revoked. Such a policy would not affect the permitted length of each stay in the United States. If any internal security risks developed, we could always revoke the visa.

By that time I had become far wiser in the ways of bureaucratic politics. I knew that my proposal would open up old battles over internal security, even if it posed no real risks. The impact of the past on the present, the importance of history, was not a matter I would again forget. By then I also knew that timing was crucial to controversial proposals. I wisely did nothing to create a revocable visa of indefinite duration until a balance-of-payments crisis led the president to seek proposals for expanding trade and travel to the United States. I had learned that the power that some executive officials and legislators have with others must be earned and then used in the formulation of alliances. And so I relied importantly on the help of my subordinate, the director of the Visa Office, who had far more influence with legislators who could block my proposal than I had.

I saw the importance of the design of the proposal; it would seem less threatening if the visa had to be re-stamped in the foreigner's passport whenever the passport expired. I recognized a far wider range of concerns of officials in the executive and legislative branch; and I studied the relations among these concerns. The representative whose opposition I most feared (because of his subcommittee chairmanship and his very conservative views) cared about more than internal security; he wanted to be consulted and treated as a central player, and he wanted to be seen as cooperating with the president's efforts to deal with the balance of payments. The secretary of state would worry about the change only so long as that most conservative congressman opposed it.

Finally, I had seen my own stakes and designed a plan of action around them. I wanted a working, regularly used addition to the system of visas, not a liberal symbol. That would require the unforced enthusiasm and support of the head of the Visa Office. I wanted a change that would last. Early consensus among liberals and conservatives and a developing constituency of literally millions of foreigners holding indefinite visas would tend to assure this result. I wanted to improve the atmosphere for sensible reductions in other travel restrictions. I could see that a visa good for at least as long as the life of a foreigner's passport—as much as ten years— would strengthen the case for extending the life of American passports, a step taken by my successor a few years later.

And I wanted to begin to enjoy the benefits that flow from a showing of political and managerial competence: being accorded more independence and deference within the areas of my jurisdiction, having these areas expanded, being given authority and resources I previously lacked, being invited to participate actively in decisions by other government agencies that affected my jurisdiction, and even being consulted by others on matters outside the area of my responsibilities. Each of these are the implicit consequences or the explicit rewards of actions warranting the confidence, respect, deference, and occasionally fear of other important political actors. The indefinite visa helped; the confusion and disarray of the passport matter had hurt.

I had learned a good deal. But I knew something was still wrong if so much calculation and weeks of personal effort were needed to accomplish an obviously sensible regulatory change within my own jurisdiction. I was acting without the power or assurance that would have come from enjoying the confidence of the secretary of state. Without that trust, I lacked a valuable resource in dealing with others. I had put together a successful initiative without knowing the crucial legislative leaders and being able to draw on their support. The secretary of state and others would have given me far more leeway if they had had reason to believe that I could handle the congressional relationships.

More than personal knowledge and established relationships would have been required to build the resources I lacked. The secretary of state, powerful members of Congress, and interest groups would want to know what the goals and plans of the Bureau of Security and Consular Affairs were and to have those goals reflect their own views as well as mine. The politics of management is broader than bureaucratic politics and involves more than obtaining discrete favorable decisions. It requires developing a coherent, defensible strategy for the organization. I first started putting that wisdom to work a decade later when I was asked to head the Criminal Division of the Department of Justice.

The book that follows is based not only on my own government experiences but, equally important, on the scores of case studies of government officials' political and managerial actions compiled by me and my colleagues at the Kennedy School of Government and other similar schools. The subject is a special sort of politics: the politics of management. It is not the politics of getting elected, but the handling of the policy choices that are faced thereafter by unelected officials, albeit in the light of electoral politics. It is not bureaucratic politics, for a wise manager is far less interested in the techniques of winning on a particular occasion than in the techniques of guiding an organization constructively and creatively over years in a world of powerful political forces. It is not about the management tasks of organizing and controlling one's subordinates in their work; it is about the problem of maintaining legislative and public support for an agency and for the goals of its leader.

The literature in the area of my concern is often brilliant but always addressed to a somewhat different set of questions. I looked at the extensive work on private management, but it did not address the particular management question that concerned me, although I have borrowed and modified the concept of management strategy as it is set forth in Kenneth Andrews's famous book, *The Concept of Corporate Strategy*. I have read much of the excellent political science literature on legislative committees, the effects of legislative rules and procedures, the handling of constituents, pressure groups, and public opinion, and the symbolic uses of politics. But Richard Fenno, Lewis Froman, Jeffrey Pressman, David Mayhew, Thomas Reid, Arthur Maass, and even John Kingdon and Murray Edelman were addressing a somewhat different set of questions from a quite distinct, descriptive perspective. On the executive side of government, Morton Halperin and Anthony Downs have both made important contributions to the study of bureaucratic politics, but my interest begins where theirs leaves off: when bureaucratic politics becomes submerged in the longer-term, more encompassing politics of management. Graham Allison's splendid *Essence of Decision* has much to teach, but its purpose is explaining not prescribing. Hugh Heclo's study of the relations of appointees and careerists and Harold Seidman's exploration of the identity of government organizations both convey essential lessons, but each is more limited in focus.*

I decided that the way to understand—and, far more difficult, to express relatively clearly yet concisely—how an effective political actor thinks about getting results in the short run and the long run would be to examine and then generalize from a large number of actual cases. I wanted to see what categories emerged from my own experience and scores of long conversations with other political actors and from an examination of many events in varied settings. Richard Neustadt's *Presidential Power* held up a hard-to-match model, but it focused entirely on the presidency.** I was

*See Kenneth R. Andrews, *The Concept of Corporate Strategy*, 2d ed., rev. (Homewood, Ill.: Richard D. Irwin, 1971); Richard F. Fenno, Jr., *Congressmen in Committees* (Boston: Little, Brown and Co., 1973); Lewis A. Forman, Jr., *The Congressional Process* (Boston: Little, Brown and Co., 1967); Jeffrey L. Pressman. *House vs. Senate: Conflict in the Appropriations Process* (New Haven: Yale University Press, 1966); David R. Mayhew, *Congress: The Electoral Connection* (New Haven: Yale University Press, 1974); T. R. Reid, *Congressional Odyssey: The Saga of a Senate Bill* (San Francisco: W. H. Freeman, 1980); Arthur Maass, *Congress and the Common Good* (New York: Basic Books, 1983); Murray Edelman, *Politics as Symbolic Action: Mass Arousal and Quiescence* (New York: Academic Press, 1971); Morton H. Halperin et al., *Bureaucratic Politics and Foreign Policy* (Washington, D.C.: The Brookings Institution, 1974); Anthony Downs, *Inside Bureaucracy* (Boston: Little, Brown and Co., 1967); Graham T. Allison, *Essense of Decisions: Explaining the Cuban Missile Crisis* (Boston: Little, Brown and Co., 1971); Hugh Heclo, *A Government of Strangers: Executive Politics in Washington* (Washington, D.C.: The Brookings Institution, 1975); and Harold Seidman, *Politics, Position and Power* (London: Oxford University Press, 1975).

**Richard E. Neustadt, *Presidential Power: The Politics of Leadership from FDR to Carter* (New York: John Wiley and Sons, 1980).

interested in the vast body of decisions made with little if any presidential involvement. What could be learned from studying many such cases?

For the general reader, I hope to explain some of the mystery in what political actors do. For the person undertaking a new governmental responsibility, this book offers the diverse experiences of a large number of political actors as a partial substitute for learning through slow, limited, and often painful experience. At a minimum it should tell new government officials how to avoid major and common mistakes. My larger ambition is to show them how to perform effectively in an extremely complicated environment of bureaucratic, legislative, and electoral politics.

Dialogue makes ideas grow. I am indebted to a number of colleagues with whom I have discussed the ideas in this book and who have provided the encouragement that comes from a shared enthusiasm for the subject. Robert Reich of Harvard's Kennedy School of Government and Ted Marmor of Yale's School of Organization and Management deserve my special gratitude. I have also profited from discussions with Professors Richard Neustadt, Martin Linsky, and Mark Moore at the Kennedy School. The editing by Marian Neal Ash and Nancy Jackson consistently improved the text. The reader will see that I owe a good deal to the carefully researched case studies that underlie each of the chapters. They are the product of an operation that has been led for more than a decade by a succession of talented directors: Steve Hitchner, Stephanie Gould, and Dottie Robyn. The cases I have used were written by Esther Scott, Paul Starobin, David Kennedy, Ronald Beaulieu, Donald Lippincott, Mark Kleiman, Eric Stern, Nancy Dolberg, Jeanne Johns, David Whitman, James Dillon, Dennis Aftergut and Arthur Applbaum. I also owe thanks to them. With the generous permission of everyone I could reach from the case study program I have incorporated parts of their descriptions of events without quotation or attribution. Quotations not attributed to other sources should be assumed to come from the case studies. Finally there are the friends who have worked tirelessly over a manuscript too often written and rewritten—Tom Potter and Ruth Thomas—and those who have done the crucial word processing—Ruth Block, Cheryl Frost, Debra Scholl Mello, Susan Salvato, and Glenn Strickland.

PART I
The Politics
   of
   Management

1 The World of the Public Manager

One view of the operations of the executive branch of government has become so familiar that it hardly seems to have competitors. The president develops policies and themes in light of his view of national needs and in response to the electoral considerations bearing on him and his party. He must win the support of the Congress to carry out his goals. As chief executive he has the additional responsibility and burden of dealing with massive organizations having their own momentum and their own ties to the legislature. Finally, the problem of making choices and executing decisions is compounded by the somewhat independent policies and interests of his major subordinates and by the bureaucratic politics through which they exercise influence and garner power.

Even when attention focuses on bureaucratic politics or on the inertia of large organizations, the central problem is seen as how to get intelligent decisions and effective control at the center of an immense executive branch—perhaps by the White House or, analogously, by a cabinet secretary attempting to deal with lesser units. Considerations of orderly, coherent organizational structure and respect for the legitimacy of the president's electoral mandate seem to dictate this perspective. But it is not the only one.

With equal plausibility the operations of the federal government could be described in radically different terms and from a radically different perspective: a world of quite independent organizations largely steering their own course and guiding their own futures, although always required to respect whatever legal and moral obligations are imposed upon them by the Congress and the president (or bureaucratic superiors) and prudentially bound to recognize their need for continuing support from the president and the Congress. Within these constraints, in this alternative view, each organization develops its own plans and visions of the public good and of the necessary conditions for its own health and survival.

This perspective assigns a far more central role to the leaders of the hundreds of government organizations, who generally decide for themselves what must be done or provide the options, persuasion, and political support that give strength and momentum to a particular alternative placed before the president or the Congress. After all, an organization's leaders enjoy a near monopoly over crucial information about its capacity, the relationship of that capacity to the nature of the problems others want addressed, and the array of other powerful players with inconsistent views on the future of the organization. Thus the leaders are guaranteed a great influence and perhaps even a veto power over new directives.

From this second perspective, the central problem is how an organization charts its path, for most decisions about what each government organization will do (and thus what government as a whole does) are made at the organizational level. And these decisions are determined by the manager's choice of plans to "market," in light of known congressional and presidential demands, to a variety of others, all of whom have something to say about the future of the organization but none of whom can displace the manager in the ultimate decision reconciling those demands. The government manager's primary job thus becomes steering the organization into the production of a desirable set of services—desirable in terms of the choice of product itself as well as the effectiveness and efficiency of production. And the product itself is more than the services offered; it is also a public statement about what is important and whose concerns deserve attention.

In this model the government manager has one final responsibility: to maintain the health of the organization by seeing that it adjusts to new political demands. The health of the organization does not mean the well-being of its employees, but rather its capacity and credible reputation for effectively discharging its present responsibilities and for being able to take on new tasks important to powerful political forces. In many respects, then, the leaders of a government organization resemble the leaders of a private corporation. Both guide ongoing, self-conscious organizations seeking a niche in the world by finding needs they can fulfill better than their competitors.

The President's Need for Others to Set Directions

There is no need to choose between the two models of the operations of the federal government. Both have validity. My point is simply that the second model should not be ignored. Beyond its descriptive powers, it has normative force, for the president (or any bureaucratic superior) has many reasons for wanting subunit heads to adopt this perspective.

Most of the matters to be handled by the federal government simply do not bear on the president's major programs, electoral demands, and needs for legislative support. The best he can do is to make clear to those who manage government organizations the broad themes and specific proposals of his administration, the important political stakes and constituencies he will rely on to stay in office, and his need for congressional support for various initiatives (support that may be affected by the actions of a sub-cabinet or cabinet officer) and to demand respect for these concerns. But these messages will not touch most of the decisions the manager must make; and the time of White House staff should not be spent resolving matters only marginally related to what the president hopes to accomplish.

Beyond this, a sensible president simply does not want his concerns automatically to control even relevant matters. Rather he would like the manager to weigh presidential concerns intelligently against others. How far the president wants his suggestions to be carried depends on the cost of the changes they invite. Costs are more than dollars and lost services; they include such matters as an unanticipated battle with a powerful legislator or angry attacks in the media. It is appointed managers who must assess the costs of the president's suggestions. Their view of the ultimate balance and suggestions about less costly alternatives are likely to be central factors in what is done.

A person who heads a government department or bureau becomes the administration's expert on a set of crucial matters: the nature of the programs in the area, the situations with which they are intended to deal, their efficacy and failures, the capacities of the organization, and the views and powers of other interested parties who can influence the agency or the administration. The president can, in short, determine who is in charge of a federal agency, but he cannot take charge. For that he must rely on others who have more time to give concentrated attention to the crucial questions in each area. The president cannot even assess how much of what is established and customary should be changed as a result of his election and the mandate it represents. Standing both at the boundary between presidential and congressional control *and* on the border between electoral politics and historic understandings and traditions guarded by the career civil (or foreign or military) service, the appointed manager must generally manage the relationship between governmental continuity and electoral claims to change.

Similarly, presidential appointees who head organizations have and want only limited control over subunits they supervise. The same is true of the Congress and of even those committees that authorize, prohibit, direct, and fund specific activities carried on by the agency. Of course the authorizing and appropriating committees can put great pressure on a government organization to respond to particular problems; the committees or their subcommittees can give much more time to a specific area of government activity than can the president or even the White House staff. But even the relevant committees must leave much to the manager of an organization, both for constitutional reasons and as a practical matter, given limited time and staff.

The Legitimacy and Power of an Agency Head to Set New Directions

Does all this vest too much power in the hands of the managers of government organizations who, after all, were not elected? I think it does not. They are still morally responsible to the commands of their superiors, the president, and the Congress, who are well able to enforce obedience when they want it. Moreover, there are real limits on a new manager's ability to set directions for the organization; even if the manager's power is equal to that of his superiors, their combined powers may be weak compared to the forces of history and custom.

The reasons for organizational inertia are obvious. The members of an organization have developed a set of skills useful only for doing particular jobs. The organization itself has an institutional memory for only certain matters. It has standard procedures, established internal jurisdictions, and routines. The personnel have been socialized to a certain view of the problems in the area and how they should be handled. Relationships have been built with powerful legislators and interest groups. The public, interest groups, other government agencies, and political figures all feel entitled to rely on expectations of what the organization will do, and these expectations have been engendered by a history of past actions.

The newly appointed manager generally has only a limited capacity to deflect such powerful organizational momentum. His knowledge of matters crucial to the success of his plans is limited. He must rely on those who have been in the business far longer (and thus who have well-settled views) for advice on political, administrative, or technological pitfalls. He generally does not enjoy the unqualified support of his superiors, for they expect him to avoid embarrassing mistakes. In any event their help is limited, for they know even less about the problems in the area than the manager does.

Much of the manager's leverage depends on concentrating his efforts on those areas in the ongoing operation that are most responsive to his reputation and skills. But even there, the activities he might seek to change are routinely carried out by a career service loyal to the agency's traditional objectives and self-image and often allied with legislators and interest groups that share those commitments.

Anne Gorsuch, Ronald Reagan's first administrator of the Environmental Protection Agency (EPA), suffered from failure to understand this. She apparently believed that the consistency of her own views with the public pronouncements of the president and the support of his constituencies provided enough political insight and power to allow her to reverse the agency's direction by reducing its budget, changing its personnel, and sharply limiting its enforcement activities. But Gorsuch vastly underrated a number of political realities: the power of private groups with different views, the importance of the media, the indifference of crucial congressmen to the president's wishes, her dependence on her own career staff to avoid old errors, and the political power of the grand alliance that often forms against the arrogance of anyone who claims to monopolize insight or control, even in a limited area of government activity. As a result, she met with stunning reversals and imposed great political costs on the president.

Ultimately, the president is seldom willing to expend as much credit as the politically thoughtless manager would require. If someone is to be undone by an uncompromising stance and style, it will probably not be the chief executive. President Reagan asked for Gorsuch's resignation not because she was ignoring his policies but because she had failed to consider the policies and powers of others as well.

In the final analysis an appointed agency head's ability to direct a government organization comes from his ability to manage the politics that decides policy within the area of the organization's responsibilities. Politics can be any peaceful system for resolving what is to be done and who is to benefit from what is done when opinions differ among competing powers, each with some claim to legitimacy. Powerful figures in the House of Representatives and the Senate, in the press and in interest groups, in other government agencies and in the Office of Management and Budget, in the White House and in the courts, in the press and on the EPA staff—all compete to control what is done with the resources and authority of the Environmental Protection Agency and, more broadly, within the area of concerns that center on the jurisdiction of the EPA. The job of the EPA administrator is to manage these politics and produce from them a coherent set of policies. He will not be allowed to become a dictator whose absolute powers are to be feared or even a field commander for the president.

The Obligations of the Manager

Clearly the responsibilities of the head of any sizable governmental unit are far more extensive than merely carrying out his superior's orders. Rather he must help the organization find its own way, subject to requirements of orderly, hierarchical structures of decision and to the electoral mandate of the president. Because they are not closely familiar with the problems the agency handles or with its capacities, neither the president nor other superiors can specify what they want in detail. Moreover, they lack necessary knowledge of the wishes and maneuvers of the other individuals and organizations that can affect the welfare of the agency and its capacity to implement policy.

Even in principle, the obligations of the manager and the organization to superiors are not always overriding. They have prior obligations to the law—that is, to the previous acts of the legislature—and to the decisions of courts. Finally, the organization embodies and maintains traditions, values, relationships, and concerns on which other organizations and individuals rely and which may be a vital part of the political fabric of the country.

William Ruckelshaus recognized all this when, on May 18, 1983, he succeeded Anne Gorsuch as the administrator of the Environmental Protection Agency. He had been EPA's first administrator from 1970 to 1973.

After that he had served briefly as acting director of the FBI and then as deputy attorney general until he was fired, as part of the Saturday Night Massacre, for refusing to execute President Nixon's order to discharge Special Watergate Prosecutor Archibald Cox. Ruckelshaus thus brought to the position a remarkable reputation for courage and integrity as well as a history of support for the Environmental Protection Agency. It is hard to say whether these assets were more needed by the organization or the president who persuaded him to come.

President Reagan faced an election a year and a half after Ruckelshaus's arrival. Polls showed that a sizable majority of the population was concerned about environmental issues and believed that Reagan was more interested in protecting polluting industries and corporations than in preserving environmental integrity. His campaign speeches had stated as much. The actions of Anne Gorsuch and of David Stockman, director of the Office of Management and Budget, removed any remaining doubt.

Under Gorsuch the EPA's senior career staff had been decimated and the vast majority of its personnel demoralized. Senior staff dedicated to environmentalist objectives had found themselves on a political "hit list." At the same time overall EPA personnel levels had been cut by about 27 percent, with particularly severe cuts in scientific personnel. The overall budget was down by 22 percent, research and development by 50 percent. Enforcement actions, especially in the area of water pollution, were virtually at a standstill as a result of Gorsuch's policy decisions, presumably supported by the White House staff. Little effort was made to deal with hazardous waste sites and other dramatic new problems. Relations with Congress and the press were as bad as these can get, and environmental groups were extremely hostile. Even regulated industries were far from pleased, because they feared the political backlash from EPA's abrupt withdrawal from any effective environmental role.

By the time he resigned shortly after President Reagan's overwhelming reelection in 1984, Ruckelshaus had lifted a heavy political liability from the president's back by reviving EPA's health, spirit, and sense of organizational integrity. Most of the steps he took were straightforward: securing an increase in the budget; removing officials openly hostile to environmental protection; promising the agency independence and support in its effort to reduce dangerous pollutants; bringing back careerists and other professionals who cared about that mission and the EPA; reestablishing vigorous enforcement; opening the agency to contact with the press and establishing a new working relationship with environmental-minded committees on the hill, and so on. Some of his actions were less obvious, such as fighting a predictably losing battle for the president's support of a several-billion-dollar program to control acid rain—a battle that told everyone concerned about the environment where Ruckelshaus and the EPA stood.

In Shakespeare's *King John* the monarch remarks, "It is the curse of Kings to be attended by slaves that take their humors for a warrant to break within the bloody house of life." It is the curse of presidents to be attended by loyalists and enthusiasts who think their duty is solely that of service to the president. As the contrast between Ruckelshaus and Gorsuch indicates, superiors are often far better served by those who recognize that they are at the center of a complex web of powers and obligations and that with centrality comes responsibility. Every sensible president wants respect for his major goals, the particular initiatives affecting an agency, his general themes as to how things will be done, and his electoral and legislative alliances. But a confident president recognizes that he is only a part, though a very major part, of a government of widely shared powers with very different webs and complexes of authority, influence, and concerns characterizing each of hundreds of policy areas. A confident president fears the curse of being attended by slaves more than the risks of sharing power with strong appointees of his own choosing and subject to his own powers of dismissal.

The Questions the Manager Must Address

The chapters that follow seek to provide some guidance to the government manager responsible for an organization operating in this complicated context of relationships. As a framework for the manager's job, I propose a set of questions.

The manager can influence the activities in which the organization engages, the themes that characterize its way of carrying out these activities, and the alliances to which it turns for support. Thus the first question is, how does the manager think about choosing the "goals" (I shall use that term to include activities, themes, and alliances) that can create a healthy organization?

Choosing once is not enough, for times will change and demand changes in goals. How does the manager monitor and recognize such new demands? And when the political world becomes less sympathetic to his goals, how can he change direction or pace without losing the support of those who share his goals and look to him for leadership?

The manager's superiors and the president (ultimately his only source of electoral legitimacy) have their own goals they want the organization to execute and express. What does the manager owe to his superiors and how does this relate to a sensible view of the independence of judgment they also want from him?

One thing superiors do *not* want is a prolonged attack in the press of the sort Anne Gorsuch generated. To avoid such an assault, the manager must recognize the areas of vulnerability in his organization and their relationship to internal management decisions, taking seriously both appearances and realities, and seeing that there are others whose views of the public welfare and personal interest will lead them to exploit organizational vulnerabilities.

Healthy organizations are more than conglomerates. How does an organization maintain and express a unified identity despite changes in administration, and why is this important? On the other hand, how does an organization express what is unique to a new administration?

How does the manager relate the goals and activities of his organization to those of other organizations working in the same area?

Finally, a manager will inevitably make some decisions with which other powerful figures do not agree. Whether or not they accept those decisions depends in part on their sense of the legitimacy of the process through which decisions were made. Should a controversial decision be presented as one that carried out the president's wishes, or as an interpretation of legislation, or as an effort to compromise between the differing views of the executive and legislative branches? Much may turn on the answer.

In the discussion that follows I provide dozens of illustrations of executive officials addressing this set of questions. Each traces what an official did and what he might have done better in a specific situation. The examples demonstrate the importance of the individuals and organizations that surround the manager of a government organization, and they provide some evidence on the central relevance of the set of questions I have just reviewed. They take the questions much further in a single setting and thus demonstrate how the manager could and should have considered her situation. But though I hope to sensitize readers' fingertips, I cannot provide the combination to the safe of political wisdom. It changes too often; one's best chance is to develop a feel for the tumblers.

2 Strategy for a Government Organization

This book is about how the person appointed by the president can come to recognize the opportunities, dangers, and obligations involved in choosing the directions and defining the identity of the organization he has been asked to head. The most important decisions are those that determine what the agency will do or what governmental and social values it will express. These decisions create alliances with interest groups and legislators. They relate closely to the goals and themes on which the president has run and may run again. They speak to broad publics about what that very important teacher, the government, believes is important and who it believes deserves respect or concern.

Goals is as good a word as any to describe decisions—visions—about what is to be accomplished, what and who is important and why, and what alliances will form the political networks of the agency. *Strategy* is the broader concept that includes both goals and the plans designed to bring them to reality. A few very simple notions are involved in the concept of strategy for a government agency; understanding their relationships provides a very powerful clue to how our government is run.

It is well to begin with a closer examination of the "politics" of managing a federal agency. Every organization, private or public, has its own internal politics. Subordinates or specialists control crucial information about the world and the operations they engage in. They can use this information, as well as their ability to make a project succeed or fail, in subtle contests with superiors or others over goals and directions. Superior officers control not only authority and advancement, but decisions about resources and personnel. Peers compete for respect, resources, and positions. All this is entirely obvious in the case of a large corporation; so what is so special about the "politics" of managing a government agency? To a far greater extent in government than in a private corporation, the power to control major management decisions is shared not only with superiors, colleagues, and subordinates but also with others outside the organization who also have power to shape its future and its goals. That is called democracy. Each of these outsiders has his own views of what should be done and how. There is no agreed-upon bottom line, such as profit or share of the market, to define success. Only in government is an individual's success so often measured by his ability to influence what an organization will regard as its task, not by its success in carrying out a generally accepted set of goals. Similarly, the willingness of crucial outsiders to support the agency will depend as much on their appraisals of its choice of goals as on its execution of them.

From what outsiders, unconnected with the executive branch, does a government organization need support? It needs legislative support to obtain resources and authority to carry out its activities. To assure this, it needs the active help of private individuals and groups and the media. It may also need the cooperation of state and local governments. Unlike a private business, a government agency does not get its resources from the sale of its product, and its authority does not come from its ownership of its property. Resources and authority must be won and held elsewhere. Thus, the manager of a government organization must share the divisive task of defining goals and activities with many others besides the president, the manager's other bureaucratic superiors, the career civil servants (often jealous guardians of the agency's historic roles and established relationships), and those other units of the federal government with which the organization must cooperate.

Needing help always means sharing power. The manager shares power with crucial legislators—particularly the congressional committees responsible for authorizing, overseeing, and funding his programs. He shares power with any private or governmental organization—local, state, foreign, or international—that has a role in causing or curing problems in his area of responsibility. Finally, he shares power with special interest constituencies organized to influence the president or the Congress and with a wider public that may vote in the next election and that is assumed to be responding in some never-really-understood way and degree to the media coverage of what the organization is doing or failing to do.

What the federal government does in hundreds of areas of activity is thus a result of the differing interests, beliefs, and alliances of: presidents and cabinet and subcabinet officers; committee chairmen and committee members; career civil servants, military officers, and Foreign Service officers; special interest constituencies; and local and national media. That is the bad news for the manager of an organization. The good news is that, with so many clamoring to influence the organization's direction, considerable power inevitably rests with whoever is responsible for putting together an intelligible, coherent policy out of the wishes of all these others, that is, the agency's appointed manager.

Those outside the organization whose support or opposition is crucial to the agency will decide whether to provide that support or opposition by looking first at three things: what the organization *does* that affects their interests; what its activities and language *say* about what is important in government and whose concerns or views of the national interest are to be given great weight; and what *alliances* with powerful organizations and individuals its words and actions seem intended to cement. The manager cannot attempt to satisfy all those who can exercise influence over his organization. That would be futile and also costly in terms of both coherence and his own vision of what is needed. The manager's task is rather to articulate and then to execute desirable goals, the support for which will provide the money and physical resources, the popular approval and cooperation, the recruits and collaborators, and the authority the organization needs to carry out those goals.

To be credible the goals must necessarily be ones that can be carried out by the organization. The staff must include people able and willing to work for these goals, and the organizational structures, resources, and authority must be adequate to the task. It is a lie, and one soon discovered, to promise outsiders whose support is needed that the organization will handle problems of concern to them if it lacks the capacity to do so. Indeed, the outsiders who care about the organization and the problems it addresses generally know its limitations and will not take seriously new statements of goals or intentions that presuppose nonexistent capacities.

The appointed manager, then, has a basic responsibility to discover, define, and effectuate goals that meet the social needs he, his superiors, and sometimes the president see in the area *and* that satisfy two additional criteria. First, the goals must be within the present or achievable capacity of the organization and consistent with the values that mobilize its energies. Second, at the same time, the goals must say things about the values of the manager and the organization, promise things about what it will do, and give indications of its likely alliances which, together, will bring it whatever outside support it needs in practical terms to carry out its goals.

But there is more to a strategy for a government organization than just a choice of goals. The manager must have plans to attain his goals. If he proposes to do something the organization is not now capable of doing, the strategy must include a plan to provide the necessary capacity. Other actions must be chosen with a view to executing the set of activities promised and communicating the message he hopes to send to those outside, and those within, the organization.

Thus the central challenge of strategy is to make desirable goals, external support, and organizational capacities fit together. The concept is simple; its application to a rich factual context is not. In this and the following chapter the history of the Federal Trade Commission (FTC) during the early and late 1970s, under two very different managers with very different objectives at very different times, is used to illustrate the application of strategy to political and organizational realities.

The FTC in 1970

The FTC was an almost irrelevant derelict when Caspar W. Weinberger was appointed its chairman by President Nixon in 1970. Weinberger was 52, a California Republican who had been budget adviser to Governor Ronald Reagan. He was regarded as a tough manager and a fiscal conservative. Though he had no particular reputation as a consumer advocate or as a trust buster, his appointment was plainly a gesture by the newly elected president toward a consumer movement that had been flexing its muscles since Ralph Nader's emergence as a national figure in 1966. Nixon told Congress that Weinberger intended to initiate a new era of vigorous action as soon as he was confirmed by the Senate and took office.

Since its creation in 1914 the FTC had been charged with prohibiting unfair methods of competition, a responsibility expanded in 1938 to include unfair or deceptive acts or practices. Consumers as well as competitors were to be protected. In addition to these broad statements of policy, over the years the FTC had been charged with a variety of more specific forms of consumer protection, including the proper labeling of fur, wool, and other textiles. And it had a major responsibility it shared with the Department of Justice—to enforce the Clayton Act against mergers that substantially curtail competition.

With five commissioners, distributed between the two major parties, and a large professional staff, the commission did its formal work in the following manner. The staff would recommend and the commission approve the filing of complaints that would then be litigated within the agency itself before administrative law judges. The full five-person commission would review the judgment of the administrative law judge. A party who lost before the commission could appeal to the federal appellate courts and ultimately to the Supreme Court. The result of all this work, if sustained at every stage, was only an order not to continue the same unfair or deceptive practice in the future. In practice, most matters were disposed of informally.

In 1969 two reports—one by a group assembled by Ralph Nader and another by a prestigious American Bar Association (ABA) commission—concluded that the FTC had made very little of the authority granted it since 1914. Presidential study commissions had repeatedly found that FTC personnel were inferior, its personnel policies irrational, its systems for handling cases severely deficient, its goals unclear, and its operations infused with partisanship and patronage. By 1969, everyone agreed, the commission was doing very, very little and that little was concentrated in the least important areas, such as the labeling of textiles and furs. In 1969 the commission spent 11 percent of its budget on ensuring the proper labeling of textiles and furs and only 9 percent on antitrust activity under the Clayton Act.

None of this was really so surprising. Traditionally the president paid little attention to the FTC and so did its authorizing and appropriating committees, except to emphasize the interest of their chairmen in fur and textile labeling. No one had more power over the FTC than the House Appropriations Subcommittee, which handled its relatively small budget. In 1970 the subcommittee was chaired by Joe Evins from Tennessee, a state whose representatives had long dominated the Federal Trade Commission.

Times change, and public attention shifts. The circulation of *Consumer Reports* tripled from 1963 to 1968 and doubled again in the next five years, so that the publication was reaching about two million purchasers and about six million total readers of higher-than-average median income and, presumably, political activity. While the concerns of some crucial committee members such as Evins remained largely parochial in 1970, President Nixon was clearly interested in establishing contact with, and eliciting support from, a rapidly growing consumer constituency. Congress had become increasingly willing to legislate in the consumer area, beginning dramatically with auto safety legislation in 1966. Powerful representatives and senators had begun campaigning on the issue of consumer protection. Senator Warren Magnuson, chairman of the Senate Commerce Committee—the authorizing and overseeing committee for the FTC—had made consumer protection a major theme in his 1968 election effort, and it had worked well. The American Bar Association was urging more vigorous consumer protection.

The Decisions to Be Made

Weinberger and Miles Kirkpatrick, his immediate successor—for Weinberger did not remain long at the Federal Trade Commission—had three important decisions to make in the early months of the new Republican administration. The first was what to do about the claims of powerful congressmen to patronage. Shortly after Weinberger's confirmation, for example, Evins took him aside at an appropriations hearing and handed him a slip of paper with the names of three top-level FTC employees whom Evins wanted "protected." The second, closely related question was whether the commission should fire or induce the retirement of a substantial proportion of the employees whose energy and skill had so often been criticized. Demoralization and confusion would inevitably follow such housecleaning.

The third question was what priorities to set for the commission's activities. Much criticism had focused on its lack of any clear direction. The ABA commission recommended an increased emphasis on ghetto fraud. Reflecting very different concerns and appealing to very different constituencies, Weinberger and Kirkpatrick could, as an alternative, turn first to their strongest unit, which dealt with deception in national advertising. To consider possible answers to these questions, I shall begin with the general problem of strategy.

Weinberger could address these and similar decisions either separately, as discrete matters, or together, as part of a broader strategy. In either case, he had to start by clarifying his own personal objectives and his own idea of how the agency could best serve the public. And he had to give due deference to the views of President Nixon, who appointed him and plainly wanted a demonstration of commitment to and concern for the rapidly growing consumer movement. Weinberger's own view of the role of government in the economy and, equally important, the personal constituency of friends and admirers who had expectations about how he would represent them in Washington might have led him to accept a dissenting recommendation of the ABA commission: that the FTC be allowed to die on the ground that it was hopelessly mired in the smallest of politics and thus inevitably ineffective. Surely both the chairman and President Nixon would have preferred terminating the FTC to continuing to do business as usual. But the president's policies and politics and the chairman's responsibilities and ambitions dictated at least trying to revitalize the agency as a vigorous protector of consumers.

What could an objective so broadly stated—to revitalize the FTC as a vigorous protector of consumers—tell Weinberger about his three decisions? Not enough. What if he asked himself the kinds of questions about tradeoffs that a purchaser of consumer or capital goods or a policy analyst of government choice might put in light of this broad objective? Would the benefit of shedding Evins's three protegés be worth the predicted $1 million reduction in an annual appropriation of about $20 million? Would the benefit of being able to make a few hundred new appointments be worth the cost in top management time, mid-level experience, and overall morale that would come with a major turnover of staff? Would the FTC produce greater public benefits per dollar expended by attempting to reduce fraud in the slums or by concentrating on national advertising addressed to the middle class? Or what would be the most beneficial mix of both programs? Even these questions, difficult as they are to answer, leave out much that is relevant.

The desirability of any major decision depends on what other decisions are also being made. For example, the importance of an appropriations cut would depend on whether the FTC was going to emphasize a labor-intensive activity such as monitoring ghetto fraud or a labor-sparing one such as monitoring national television advertising. And the impact of any decision depends on the reactions of all those who can give or withhold support as well as on the relationship of the decision to the particular objectives the organization is to pursue; the choice of objectives decides not only what support will be needed but also what will be forthcoming. Finally, the responses of other powerful players outside and within the organization depend upon far more than their attempt to second-guess the managers' choice of tradeoffs on a particular occasion. These crucial responses turn far more importantly upon what the whole *set* of relatively visible decisions made by the managers of the organization conveys about what the activities, values, and alliances of the agency are to be. These complexities demand of the manager a more refined vision of the future of his agency, one that adds to his own and the president's hopes consideration of the likely reactions of other influential participants to alternative visions and plans—to the possible goals—for the organization.

An Integrating Vision

Goals combine judgments about what is desirable and estimates about what is possible. It is generally wise to begin with an analysis of what is possible. A feasible goal must satisfy two conditions: (1) the organization must be able and willing to carry it out; and (2) the goal must elicit whatever support is needed from those not subject to the managerial control of the organization's leaders. The second means, in Weinberger's case, that what the goal promises to accomplish, conveys about values, and invites in the way of alliances must bring the support of: the legislators who must authorize and fund the FTC's activities; the private businesses that must accept and comply with its decisions; and those individuals who must be recruited to work within the organization to carry out its purposes. In every case, there must be a congruence—a stable fit—among the manager's objectives, the internal capabilities and inclinations of the organization, and the conditions of obtaining needed outside support.

A strategy goes beyond recognition of a desirable goal that is feasible in terms of internal capacity and external support. A manager also needs to see the broad outlines of a plan for obtaining the needed capacity and support and understand the sequence of major steps leading toward carrying out his objectives. If the goal is not within the present capacity of the organization, there must be an acceptable means to develop that capacity. If the needed outside support is not there, there must be a realistic way to bring it into being. Finally, the goal and plan—that is, the strategy—must be specific enough to provide guidance on a number of matters, notably, the major priorities in activities to be undertaken by the organization and the most important organizational steps required to develop the capacities needed to carry these out. For lesser, more isolated decisions, the strategy should also provide an ability to assess their importance in relation to the overall plan and goals. A set of notions that serves these purposes would be a well-developed strategy for the organization.

Weinberger needed to recognize the FTC's possible goals and then to determine whether there was a realistic plan for moving the commission from its present goals to others he preferred. The newly chosen goals and actions had to be, within a reasonably short time, both within the capabilities of the organization and responsive to the views of those outsiders who controlled the resources the agency needed to carry out those goals. And it had to be possible to get "there" from "here;" that is, from the present state of the organization.

As we have seen, the Federal Trade Commission that Weinberger inherited had drifted into one particular form of stable relationship between its members and the outside supporters it relied upon. In the decades before 1970 it had received neither active support nor disapproval from the executive branch. Presidents had traditionally expected little from the FTC, except to avoid making waves. Its activities, such as its emphasis on fur and textile labeling, were chosen to serve the interests of powerful legislators who could provide the commission with whatever authority and funding were needed for its quite limited purposes. A few narrow economic interests also supported the activities of the commission. No powerful interest groups would attack the FTC, for it chose its adversaries carefully (with the notable exception of a brief foray against the cigarette industry in the late 1960s).

It had bolstered its support with influential representatives and senators by becoming a seat of patronage appointments. As a small agency, it did not require any more broadly based support to maintain its funding. Because it was satisfied with its statutory authority—to issue cease-and-desist orders that could be litigated for years and then merely forbid repetition of closely related wrongdoing—it did not require any further legislation. Its operating capacities were woefully weak. But it could do the very little that was required to maintain the small measure of outside support necessary for its survival.

Weinberger's search for a strategy had to begin by identifying some possible alternative states of congruence among goals, organizational capacities, and external support. Rejecting the Evins demand for patronage and departing from the emphasis on such matters as fur and textile labeling would destabilize the established balance. Whether these steps would do anything positive to serve Weinberger's goals depended upon whether there was some other form of stable equilibrium to which the commission could move and whether these actions would be useful in making that move. Any such state would require different goals, eliciting different support and carried out by a staff with different capabilities.

Weinberger could, of course, see the prospect of new forms of outside support for changed goals. His appointment by President Nixon came about as a result of major changes in conditions outside the Federal Trade Commission. Ralph Nader had created a vigorous consumer constituency during the late 1960s. The economy was strong, and Congress had given increasing attention to the concerns of consumers. The commission, which had long lacked the support of the president or Congress for any major initiatives, now was subject to demands from both for just such initiatives—demands fueled by the apparent electoral strength of the consumer movement.

Weinberger might well have asked whether such generalized support for consumer protection would elicit the specific authorizations and appropriations that would be needed for a revitalized commission. He could not be sure, but the prospects were there. No chairman of a committee or subcommittee wants to lose on the floor, and in 1970 that was a real possibility for anyone who opposed consumer initiatives, especially when as conservative an organization as the American Bar Association was behind the commission. The commerce committees of both houses would be likely to grant needed statutory changes. The appropriations committees, even Subcommittee Chairman Evins, had to look over their shoulders at a Congress anxious to respond to a large, newly self-conscious interest group— consumers.

The Implications of Adopting a New Goal

Thus a changed goal—vigorously pursuing consumer interests—might well elicit the outside support that would be needed. But giving that goal some reality in terms of effective actions would plainly require capabilities not present in the organization that Weinberger inherited. It would be necessary to bring in new people, to design new processes, and to develop new organizational structures. Much that was there would have to be dismantled, and many people might have to be discharged. Moving the Federal Trade Commission to a new stable posture with goals of consumer protection and with support from the consumer movement, Congress, and the president would require dramatic changes in the organization.

The point is important. Only certain combinations of goals, outside support, and organizational capabilities are stable. An organization with the internal traditions and capabilities of the FTC Weinberger inherited could not carry out the goals of vigorous consumer protection or maintain for long the necessary outside support. And if Weinberger publicized a shift to new goals and an appeal to new sources of outside support by rejecting demands for patronage in positions and priorities, the commission's old sources of outside support—Congressman Evins and others— would soon withdraw their assistance.

Beyond a sense of alternative equilibria, then, an organizational strategy also requires a notion of whether (and how) it is possible to move to, and maintain, a new balance among goals, outside support, and organizational capabilities. A decision to move the Federal Trade Commission toward an important role in the consumer movement had some crucial implications. Cutting off the agency's former base of political support, Weinberger would have to show promptly that the commission *deserved* to be vigorously supported by consumer advocates. The FTC would have to act soon with wholly unexpected force. Yet the reorganization of the commission, including recruitment and training of new people, would take time— far more time than consumerists might allow this long moribund agency.

To adopt a strategy centered on a new goal of vigorous consumer protection, the chairman had to choose initial actions that the agency could accomplish with its limited capabilities but that would promptly generate and maintain political support while the leadership of the commission built the internal capacities necessary for its new role. Were there such possibilities?

The alternative recommended by the American Bar Association— focusing on retail fraud in slum neighborhoods—was not promising. It satisfied neither of the two requirements: feasibility with limited capacities and prospects of generating major increased trust from consumer advocates. The commission wholly lacked the capability to handle so diffuse a problem. The results would not be dramatic or prompt; they might even be negligible. The poor and the weak could not offer political power and support; these groups played no important part in the consumer movement.

The FTC's only real strength was in the Bureau of National Advertising.

This was also the area where highly visible initiatives could be taken that would be recognized by members of a movement characterized by middle-class status and an orientation toward large national issues involving major industries. The new steps could include requests for expanded legislative authority, such as stronger sanctions and an ability to make rules to deal wholesale with consumer problems. Other initiatives could involve more imaginative use of present delegated authority: new requirements of affirmative disclosure of product information, standardization of warranties, or increased protection for vulnerable groups such as the aged and children. Such initiatives might convince the consumer movement of the FTC's importance, and the movement in turn might enlist congressional and maintain presidential support.

Weinberger had no guarantee that this strategy would succeed or would succeed quickly enough. But its prospects were more attractive than the alternatives. Allowing the organization to dwindle slowly into obscurity (as Richard Posner, the dissenter on the ABA commission, had recommended) would frustrate the president's desire to show support for the consumer movement. Still less appealing was the second alternative: to continue business as usual, trading jobs and unimportant activities for the support of a few strategically placed legislators. Thus the bold outlines of a strategy for Weinberger seemed clear.

What did this strategy tell him about how to handle the Evins note requesting the retention of three top managers—a matter that had been left quite indeterminate? The Evins "request" required a major decision, both symbolically and practically. Accepting Evins's directives would signal that the agency was continuing with a strategy very much like that of the past. Those working in the organization would be uncertain as to who was in control and whether the long-established way of doing business would be changed. So would Evins. On the other hand, stating simply and powerfully that the commission would no longer do business as usual would be useful, almost essential, to changing the traditions of the organization. It would also be useful as a way of conveying to Nader, the ABA, and legislators concerned about consumer interests that the agency was traveling a new path. And strategies must be conveyed by actions, not by words; old hands will watch what is done, not what is said.

Weinberger ignored the Evins "request" and proceeded to reorganize as he saw fit, placing his own people where he thought they were needed and removing others, including those supported by Evins. Once one understands the strategic choices, this decision becomes obvious. Although the commission's appropriations were cut in retaliation, Weinberger had marked off a new path toward congressional support and begun the house-cleaning necessary to keep that support in future years. As the next chapter shows, his boldness was amply rewarded.

3 *Strategy and Leadership*

If democracy is to work, governmental organizations must change directions as public opinion, legislative opinion, and power shift. Such a shift, of dramatic proportions, had taken place in the area of consumer concerns shortly before Casper Weinberger was appointed chairman of the Federal Trade Commission in 1970. Another, counterrevolutionary shift was to take place under the feet of Mike Pertschuk, who was appointed chairman of the FTC in 1977. If strategy works as an integrating, organizing concept, it should be applicable to retrenchment as well as to expansion, to 1977 as well as to 1970. It is. But implementation in this context of retrenchment presents particular problems for a manager because it may undermine the personal support on which he depends.

Changes at the FTC, 1970–77

In his eight months as chairman of the FTC (before moving to the Office of Management and Budget), Casper Weinberger reorganized the agency into five "missions." But the real organizational change took place beneath the surface. Basil Mezines, an FTC veteran who became Weinberger's executive director, helped the new chairman weed out incompetent and unproductive staff; a significant number were fired, demoted, transferred, or (most commonly) encouraged to retire. By the spring of 1971, eighteen of thirty-one top staff members had left the agency; about 200 of the nearly 600 middle- and lower-level staff attorneys had also cleaned out their desks.

After Weinberger's departure, the commission began writing on the slate he had succeeded in wiping clean. His successors—Miles Kirkpatrick, Lewis Engman, and Calvin Collier—undertook a vigorous recruiting effort to staff the FTC with bright, aggressive, young attorneys. By 1977 the agency had relatively few seasoned middle managers and many talented, green, and highly volatile line attorneys. The turnover rate was high, for FTC salaries could not match those of the private sector.

Between 1970 and 1977, FTC activities became increasingly forceful. The Bureau of Competition, for example, moved steadily from an emphasis on monopolistic conduct to monopolistic structure. Previously, the mainstay of the bureau had been penny-ante price discrimination cases under the Robinson-Patman Act. In 1967, 173 investigations of violations of the Robinson-Patman Act were initiated; by 1976, that number had been reduced to 6. The bureau was going after larger game, aiming at the structural sources of market power. Under the novel theory of "shared monopoly," the FTC undertook mammoth actions against two oligopolies: the four largest breakfast cereal manufacturers and the eight largest petroleum refiners.

The changes in the consumer protection effort were even more radical. Prosecution under the Wool and Fur Product Labeling Acts virtually ceased, and the agency abruptly moved away from nickel-and-dime cases drawn from the mailbags. Deceptive national advertising became the bold new focus: the FTC took on the questionable claims of WonderBread, Bufferin, Excedrine, and Listerine. It developed two new weapons in the advertising campaign: (1) an ad substantiation program, putting the burden of documentation of claims squarely on the shoulders of the advertisers; and (2) a doctrine of corrective advertising, a bold legal remedy that survived numerous court challenges.

The passage of the Magnuson-Moss Act in 1975 substantially extended the reach of the FTC's regulatory arm by adding industry-wide rulemaking authority. Previously, the agency's major regulatory weapon had been the cease-and-desist order, issued to a particular firm found to have done something unfair or deceptive, after an adjudicative proceeding. Now the commission could announce in advance, after a legislative-type hearing, what fairness or honesty required in an entire industry's advertising or other sales practices.

Pertschuk's Republican predecessors eagerly set out to exercise the FTC's new authority. In one eight-month period, fourteen consumer protection rule-making proceedings were initiated. When Pertschuk took over in 1977, he inherited seventeen pending ventures that cut a broad swath across the American market: the FTC had taken on funeral practices, used cars, credit practices, over-the-counter drugs, eyeglasses, mobile homes, hearing aids, food advertising, health spas, vocational schools, flammable plastics, appliance labeling, protein supplements, care labeling, franchises, home insulation materials, and gasoline station lotteries.

The Federal Trade Commission, as a matter of practice, initially drafted its proposed rules in very broad, ambitious terms—frightening to the industries they would regulate—assuming that the rules would later be narrowed in response to the comments of the industries affected by them. In 1977 most of the prospective rules were still at least a year away from final promulgation and had not yet been revised in response to public scrutiny.

The Objectives And Constituencies of the New Chairman

Mike Pertschuk was appointed chairman of the FTC by President Carter in March 1977. One of a number of liberal, public interest advocates appointed to subcabinet posts, Pertschuk had been the chief counsel to the powerful Senate Commerce Committee for six years and a committee staffer for seven years before that. Carter promised Pertschuk independence from White House interference, expected in turn that Pertschuk would demonstrate independence from personalities on the hill, and encouraged him to pursue vigorously the interests of the consumer.

The encouragement was hardly necessary. Every significant consumer group in Washington already recognized that Mike Pertschuk was the accomplished leader in the consumer field. This was important. Appointed officials, like elected officials, have their own constituencies, separate from those of the agencies they head. Appointees thrive when they are supported by others who accept them as representatives of their interests and beliefs. The influence of such constituencies flows from a mixture of political resources, psychological tensions when close friends or allies differ fundamentally about wise public policy, and the official's concern about his personal reputation outside governmental circles. Each of these strands has considerable independent strength. Intertwined, they explain a great deal about the behavior of a political actor.

Consider the third strand. Often an extremely important factor in the decisions of an appointed official is a desire to remain a respected member and leader of some group, outside the government, with generally similar beliefs about government policy. Conscience was one of the reasons that Elliott Richardson would not fire Archibald Cox at President Nixon's behest during the Watergate period. But, as one talented reporter noted, another reason, closely related to conscience, was that there were no bases for this action acceptable to the friends and associates in Boston and Washington whose opinions he valued and from whom he would want respect for years to come. Similarly, President Reagan's secretary of the interior, James Watt, who had previously identified himself with very conservative groups, could not take positions antithetical to his supporters without bearing considerable personal costs. That both men were doubtless powerfully motivated by conscience or belief does not weaken the claim that personal constituencies are potent forces. Conscience and belief are social as well as individual phenomena.

The other strands are also powerful. Practical, political considerations may strongly reinforce the influence of such private, issue-based constituencies. A manager may have been appointed as much to satisfy an issue constituency as for the country at large; he or she may have been chosen primarily as spokesperson for a set of beliefs rather than for capacities for management. Appointed officials remember why they were appointed. And it is hard, psychologically, to depart from the values, beliefs, and expectations of friends and supporters.

An appointed official in the executive branch also has organizational constituencies, of course: the people in the unit he heads, the organized groups that support and defend its traditional activities, its loyalists on the hill, and the larger department to which it belongs. With the job come powerful expectations about what he should value, what he will believe, and how he will behave. His need for support of every sort creates the motivation to honor those expectations too. At times the expectations of personal constituencies are inconsistent with those of organizational constituencies. Those who supported the appointment of Anne Gorsuch to head the Environmental Protection Agency expected actions abhorrent to the supporters of the EPA. Those who supported President Reagan's early choices to the board of the Legal Services Corporation demanded actions that the supporters of legal services would resist passionately. The question for the manager then becomes whether to desert personal supporters or struggle against agency constituencies to reverse the direction of the agency. No decision is more painful.

Even if the manager's own views, the reason for his appointment, his personal supporters, and organizational constituencies all press for movement in the same direction, as was true for Mike Pertschuk, other risks may await him. The rest of the politically relevant world may not agree with the direction. Often everything depends on this hard-to-detect matter of public and political receptivity. When the broader political climate is in accord with the goals shared by a manager, his personal and organizational constituencies, and the president—that is surely a time for pushing ahead dramatically. Such a happy constellation of forces rarely coalesces to support an issue and its advocates except after a lopsided election. President Johnson's "War on Poverty" rode such a wave in 1965; President Reagan's war on government and taxation spent much of its force in a few short months in 1981. To hesitate at such a time is to invite the righteous anger of supporters who have patiently awaited the fleeting moment of opportunity. The election of President Carter in the aftermath of the corporate wrongdoing revealed by the Watergate investigations may have looked like such an opportunity to consumerists and environmentalists. If so, it was fleeting indeed.

Pertschuk had to observe carefully and decide whether the times were indeed right for headlong consumerist advances, for misjudgment risked disaster. If the manager forcefully pushes his agency's powers to their legal limits on behalf of goals for which outside support is lacking, his opponents will mount charges of illegitimacy and overreaching. And his very vigor, command, and clarity of direction will help others rally around opposition to both his actions and his views about what and who are good or bad, right or wrong, important or to be ignored.

Changing Times: Politics and the Business Community

In Weinberger's time and for several years after, support for vigorous consumer initiatives undertaken by the Federal Trade Commission was secure. The consumer movement was strong, its opposition weak. This situation was changing dramatically in the last half of the 1970s. The consensus favoring governmental activity in the realm of consumer protection was dissipating. The numbers of those in Congress committed to the consumer movement had dwindled. Their advantages from occupying key positions were also less significant than they had once been. The organization of consumer interests into a politically formidable constituency had faltered; opposing interests were showing increasing political muscle. All this should have been obvious in 1977 and 1978.

The fate of proposed consumer legislation provided some unmistakable signs. In late 1977 efforts to obtain a Consumer Protection Agency failed, though the measure had passed the House with a 300-vote margin five years earlier. A hardly less obvious warning was the changing composition of Congress. Gone were many of the most devoted supporters of the consumer movement, including Senators Phil Hart, John Pastore, John Moss, John Tunney, and Dick Clark. The powerful staff of the Senate Commerce Committee, devoted supporters of the consumer movement in the mid-1970s, was now dispersed. The chairmanship had recently shifted from the consumerist Warren Magnuson to the less enthusiastic Howard Cannon. A conservative tide had already begun to win seats in both houses. A number of senators and representatives who were strong supporters of the consumer movement had lost elections at a time when business political action committees (PACs) were contributing substantial amounts of money to their opponents. Other members were getting the message.

All of this would have had less dramatic results in a Congress still controlled by powerful committee chairmen, for in the House and Senate they were sympathetic to the Federal Trade Commission. But the structure of Congress had changed in the years since Caspar Weinberger was chairman. The power of committees had declined. Well-financed special interests had learned how to use money and grassroots lobbying to produce rebellious majorities on the floor.

Members of Congress with waning consumerist sympathies found themselves courted by a business community that had rewritten the rules of industrial lobbying. The formation in 1972 of the Business Roundtable, a periodic meeting of the nation's top chief executive officers, sparked an awareness of the possibilities of cooperation among firms. As David Dunn, a lobbyist with the Patton, Boggs, and Blow firm, commented: "If you put ten different companies or ten different trade associations in one room you're bound to have a plant in a lot more Congressional districts and a lot more states than if you're just one person."

By the time industry and the Carter White House joined battle in 1977 over the latest (and last) attempt to create a consumer agency, business had transformed its ways of pursuing its interests. An attorney whose law firm handled over three-quarters of the FTC trade rule regulations remembered that, "For the first time in history, you had 'the coalition': National Association of Manufacturers, Grocery Manufacturers of America, the U.S. Chamber of Commerce, National Federation of Independent Business, all together, and thousands of people underneath them, in a highly structured, organized way, taking positions, moving, dividing up the Hill, and lobbying. Tremendous power was brought to bear."

If committees enjoyed less deference, administrative and executive agencies were encountering congressional hostility in the aftermath of Watergate, Vietnam, and presidential refusals to spend appropriated sums (impoundments). Congress was determined to reassert its control over the executive. Perhaps the legislature had run out of new initiatives, especially in light of growing public disillusionment with government. In any event, strong oversight of executive activities had become a dominant theme of legislative activity. Pertschuk, an expert on the Congress, should have seen the danger in all this.

Pertschuk should also have recognized a broader framework for these changes. Widely held beliefs and attitudes were shifting. Pertschuk came to the FTC in a period of general loss of faith in the ability of government to solve major problems. Too many promises of the Great Society period, both social programs and regulatory initiatives, had been unmet. At the same time, encouraged by the academic work of well-funded conservative think-tanks, arguments for less government and for deregulation of business were developing currency, legitimacy, and acceptance.

Congress had taken the first steps toward a broader policy of deregulation with a vigorous attack on the Civil Aeronautics Board led, significantly, by Senator Edward Kennedy and other liberals. They set a precedent of support for deregulation in one context (rates and markets) that proved hard to disavow in other areas (such as consumer or environmental protection). The media were also becoming less interested in the consumer movement; Ralph Nader seemed to be wearing thin.

Behind all these changes lay a dramatic difference in the economy. It had turned sour. Inflation was rampant, productivity gains were slight. It was not the time, many thought, to impose additional burdens on business.

The new organizational strength of business strongly reinforced the trend of decreasing support for governmental regulation. Business lobbies now combined the power of broad coalitions of interest groups with the effective use of campaign contributions *and* grassroots lobbying. The apparent weakness of the liberal opposition and heightened hopes of conservative success bolstered business groups' attacks on governmental interference. Labor's major concerns in a time of faltering economy were in areas of employment, not consumer issues. The media had lost interest. Many leaders of the consumer movement had joined the Carter administration, leaving citizen groups anemic. Consumerist opposition to business interests began to look like a paper tiger.

Three Decisions Facing Pertschuk

In May 1977, the House and Senate commerce committees began to consider HR 3816, the FTC Improvements Act, which also contained a three-year authorization amendment. The bill, which would broaden significantly the powers of the FTC beyond those granted by Magnuson-Moss, had two particularly controversial provisions: *class action suits,* permitting groups and individuals to seek redress for violations of the FTC rulings in the courts; and *equitable relief,* authorizing the FTC to petition the courts to place in receivership companies facing FTC penalties that were likely to dissipate their assets.

The bill was received warmly at the subcommittee and committee levels in both the House and the Senate, with both committees reporting similar bills that were extremely favorable to the FTC. But the situation was very different when the House bill reached the floor on October 3, 1977. Overwhelming majorities stripped away the new powers. Ten days later, the House was considering an even more severe rebuke to the agency, in the form of a legislative veto amendment offered by Jim Broyhill (R–N.C.). The amendment called for the so-called one-house veto: if one house voted its disapproval of any new FTC rule, and the other at least acquiesced, the rule making would be void. The Broyhill proposal carried handily. When the Senate insisted on removing the legislative veto at conference in February 1978, the House responded by rejecting the conference report.

In these early, troubled months as chairman, Pertschuk faced several crucial decisions about the FTC's activities, organization, and alliances.

ACTIVITIES

The notorious weakness of the commission's traditional remedy—issuance of a cease-and-desist order to a single company—had led to the passage of the Magnuson-Moss Act allowing the promulgation of rules binding on many parties. Filled with enthusiasm for this badly needed source of new authority, Pertschuk's predecessors had, in more favorable times, initiated a substantial number of rule-making proceedings, each of which would have been regarded by the Congress itself as a major legislative step. Each rule had the effect of organizing a substantial constituency scattered throughout the country into active opposition. The combination of rules, largely directed at small businesses, which had previously been the beneficiaries of FTC action, revived the Chamber of Commerce as an effective and hostile lobbying body.

Proceeding by way of adjudication in individual cases had the effect, before the Magnuson-Moss Act, of isolating the particular target, as a wrong-doer, from the rest of its industry. The new rule-making proceedings, in contrast, tended to unify the members of an industry, sometimes several industries, in organized opposition to the rule. Pertschuk's predecessors had planted the seeds of politically sensitive rules, but they were now beginning to sprout above the ground, and their timing was apparently out of control. Every government manager is the inheritor of the fruits of his predecessors' initiatives. Momentum comes with the job.

The massive shifts in the world to which the Federal Trade Commission had to look for its outside support rather plainly posed the following choice to Mike Pertschuk as the commission's chairman. He could follow the bold path of exercising fully the powers to make industry-wide rules that Congress had granted the commission in the Magnuson-Moss Act of 1975. Or he could proceed with substantial caution on the theory that those powers were too valuable to risk at a time when the tide had turned sharply against consumers. The first path would mean, at a minimum, carrying through on the promises of the first seventeen rules that Pertschuk had inherited from his predecessors.

The bold path could be, and was, carried further. Motivated by conscience and a desire to make his own mark and reassure his consumerist constituency, Pertschuk quickly set his staff to work on a bold additional rule-making initiative known as "kid-vid": a proposed rule-making process designed to regulate television advertising directed at children. The most extreme of the alternatives being considered was a flat ban on any advertising directed toward children below the age of eight. At stake was the economic impact of $600 million of children's advertising revenues and the business interests it represented: broadcasters, advertisers, cereal manufacturers, grocery businesses, and sugar concerns.

The gains from following the bold path depended upon whether Congress would allow such rules to stand. If it did, consumers would enjoy an array of new protections, and precedents would have been set establishing the legitimacy and wide boundaries of the commission's new powers. The victories would presumably strengthen the enthusiasm of two groups that were important to Pertschuk: the staff of the commission itself and the consumerist organizations outside. But if Congress rejected the commission's new rules, the costs could be very great. The commission's most valued power—the new rule-making authority—was at stake, not just the results of its exercise in the particular cases at hand.

At a minimum, organized business interests would learn that the commission could be defeated in Congress. The success of one group would encourage other targets of regulation to organize allies and would strengthen their hand in Congress, where attacks are far more likely on individuals, organizations, and programs already shown to be vulnerable. Beyond that, opponents in Congress might want to send a message as clear as a restriction on the commission's rule-making powers.

These risks could be reduced only by proceeding with obvious restraint in promulgating new rules. But such restraint amounted to reining in the enthusiasm of the consumer groups and the young, dedicated staff of the Federal Trade Commission. This too would have its costs.

If it was clear that the powers of the commission were likely to be severely restricted either by legislation or by the threat of legislation, then the chance of great damage to consumerism plainly dictated a change in strategy. Bold, imaginative, daring leadership in pressing new rules and regulations would risk too much for too little chance of some gains.

ORGANIZATION

Pertschuk also had to decide during these early months what to do about the two centers of organizational controversy *within* the FTC: the cautious General Counsel's Office and the free-market-minded, skeptical Office of Policy Planning. These offices had been serious irritants to the more imaginative and dedicated consumerists who now dominated the FTC. Pertschuk and his predecessors had hired a staff committed to consumer advocacy, and Pertschuk had instilled in them a camaraderie based on the enthusiasm of warriors united against powerful adversaries. To strengthen their cohesiveness and their determination, he could reduce the sources of internal dissent. The General Counsel's Office could be told to stay out of discussions of policy. The Office of Policy Planning could be instructed to get along better with the operating bureaus, muting its sharp economics-based criticism.

But these steps, while strengthening cohesion, would also eliminate the natural centers of attentiveness to the business world and its academic and lawyer allies. This would be especially dangerous now, because communication with the commission had already been made difficult. In the aftermath of Watergate, Pertschuk had established strict rules concerning informal contacts with parties involved in any decision before the commission and had cut himself off from the close relationships with the Washington bar that had previously sped the flow of information and criticism from outside the agency. Steps taken to prevent undue influence by parties who would be affected by commission actions had, at the same time, denied the commission firsthand experience of the strength of others' reaction to its proposals.

Pertschuk's organizational decisions were consistent with creating a high-spirited, one-sided advocacy agency. Such a creation may be appropriate on those rare occasions when the external world is clearly very supportive, but when it is hostile—or even must be watched for changing sympathies—the single-minded, pre-set organization promises thoughtless, uncalculating conflict with needed sources of external support.

ALLIANCES

Finally, Pertschuk had to choose the language of his stewardship, the statements of goals and visions that would shape the alliances for and against the FTC. Here one path was to speak, in the clearest language, of the dangers of giving profit-minded business its head and to promise, unequivocally, the agency's firm commitment to strengthening the powers of consumers in the marketplace. Consumer groups would then have their leader, but businesses and industries would be driven to mobilize promptly to contest the powers of the FTC in their own defense. Each group would turn to Congress but, in the wake of a failing economy and a conservative tide, the business groups would have a far more sympathetic hearing.

The alternative, to speak in more neutral terms that conveyed respect for the integrity of most businesses and for the general efficiency of the marketplace, might confuse Pertschuk's more impassioned supporters but would reassure and demobilize some potential opponents and neutralize their arguments. It would also draw support from the claims of quasi-judicial neutrality that surround some decisions made by administrative agencies.

If he decided to press forward vigorously with the consumerist agenda, honesty might demand forthrightness about his strategy. But he could still decide not to announce his plans long in advance. His fighting words could wait to accompany his decisions and actions, at least if he could still make clear to his staff what he expected of them.

Pertschuk's Strategic Choices

What should Mike Pertschuk's strategy have been in this situation? The crucial facts were: (1) that his agency's external support was fading fast while its opposition was strengthening; but (2) that retreat on his part threatened both his own support and the dedication of his staff and the commission's outside allies. Pertschuk's fundamental responsibility to his cause and constituency was to maintain intact as much of the consumer movement's crucial assets as possible in the face of the gathering storm. Prominent among those assets were: the commitment of dedicated individuals like Ralph Nader and his followers throughout the country; the support of mass publics, often nourished by media sympathy for consumer issues; allies on the hill and in the White House; and the legal powers and the authorized and funded staff of the FTC. His responsibility to shift, to the advantage of consumers, the lines that demarcate and separate the areas of consumer protections and business freedoms was secondary.

Pertschuk's fundamental objective for the FTC should have been to maintain its values, solidarity, powers, and staffing in a time of extreme and determined assault on its authority and activities. This would be no small task. His concern for new powers or growth, like his concern for new substantive advances in the marketplace, would have to wait.

If the heart of Weinberger's plan was to get out in front of a budding consumer movement and, as quickly as possible, create the staff and obtain the powers necessary to maintain that position, the heart of Pertschuk's strategy should have been to slow down an agency too far ahead of its support without losing the loyalty and commitment of its talented consumerist staff. This would require Pertschuk to disappoint his personal constituency, as Weinberger may have disappointed his. But the cost of fully exercising and even stretching the new powers of the commission on behalf of concrete consumer gains would be to help organize a powerful opposition, to subject Pertschuk's supporters to effective public attacks and legislative defeat, and to run the risk that valuable powers would be cut back sharply by Congress. The risks were obviously so grave as to out-weigh the chance of making further dramatic gains for the consumer movement.

Pertschuk in fact led the organization in a very different, far less cautious direction—attempting to maintain and build upon its bold leadership in consumerist causes. He silenced the internal criticism of his dissenting offices. He accelerated the process of rule making. And he announced his loyalties in clearly adversarial, consumerist terms. No one now argues that the results of Pertschuk's boldness and vigor were desirable. He, like others, recognizes that they encouraged and strengthened the cause of organized business interests as they brought their weight to bear on an increasingly conservative Congress. The result was a series of actions in which Congress indicated unmistakably that it felt that the Federal Trade Commission was overreaching in its claim of powers and threatened legislative withdrawal of the new rule-making power. But hindsight is too easy. My claim is that a careful reflection on the politics of management would have revealed the dangers and suggested a different path.

An organization cannot long continue to pursue goals that no longer enjoy the support, or at least tolerance, of those who provide the resources and authority it needs. These essentials are only loaned, not given, to the organization by Congress and the president. A public manager who sees changes in the political context that may undermine his support must modify some activities if necessary to maintain adequate support for more important ones. He may even have to rethink goals and strategies.

An expanded use of rule-making procedures was so fundamental to Pertschuk's goals and those of his supporters that broadly abandoning the proposed rules might well have demoralized the organization. Perhaps most of the many rule-making proceedings had to continue. But some of them and other actions might well have been adjusted radically in light of the changing environment for consumer protection. Pertschuk took an opposite direction; undaunted, he pressed forward with stunning boldness. Adding the children's television rule-making proceeding (''kid-vid'') to the barrage of other rules brought the giants of merchandising, advertising, and the media to an already powerful opposition based largely on the small business community. However desirable it was to regulate advertising on children's television, Pertschuk's initiative had only a limited chance of surviving congressional assault and was sure to provoke a far broader and more effective attack on everything the commission was doing.

At the same time—pursuant to the same strategy—the chairman spoke out in very bold language with unmistakable meaning. No one could think that he was neutral on the questions of business freedom and consumer protection. He described the FTC as an agency that should and would side with the consumer to the maximum extent possible. He did not trust business or the unregulated marketplace. And these views were, not surprisingly, reflected in staff attitudes. Highly adversarial and irritating to those on the outside, the staff planted the seeds of paranoia in business interests already excluded from familiar forms of contact with the commission.

Obviously it is a condition of effective leadership that the goals set and activities pursued must not be such as to generate an effective demand for limitation of the manager's responsibility. Yet this was rather obviously where Pertschuk's strategy was leading. His proposed rules for children's television seemed the last and most extreme of a set of measures running directly contrary to the tide of congressional and popular beliefs: that there was far too much regulation of business. Such a widely shared congressional consensus on the direction of governmental activity is rare, except following a presidential election, a crisis, or a notable failure. When present, it is powerful. The Federal Trade Commission not only charged directly into this tide; it became a symbol of the kind of governmental activity that should be stopped.

Beyond this, powerful constituencies had organized in opposition to the FTC's activities; no roughly equal counterweight supported the commission. And the "kid-vid" proceeding had brought the media to the side of the commission's opponents and the deregulators; there was no way to call on the press to elicit public support. The only major vulnerability the commission had not created or confronted was the opposition of the leaders of its oversight, authorizing committees. Their influence, based on a superior knowledge of the commission and the congressional deference that comes with delegated responsibility, was not arrayed against Mike Pertschuk, at least not yet.

The commission was also running into serious conflict with a second requirement of maintaining a loan of responsibility and authority: legitimacy. A Congress determined to assert its own authority and to maintain control of the executive saw the boldness of the FTC's law-making initiatives as a perfect example of executive authority run amuck. The "kid-vid" initiative went well beyond traditional considerations of truth in advertising, and even beyond more recent requirements of full disclosure.

In the most sympathetic of times many in Congress and many lawyers would have questioned a claim that this was merely a quasi-judicial interpretation of the statute or one based largely on agency expertise. And these were not sympathetic times. Moreover, the chairman's declared goal of vigorous and partisan advocacy of consumer interests was flatly inconsistent with any claim of legitimacy based on a neutral, judicious application of congressional standards.

Mike Pertschuk had ignored all of the conditions of claiming legitimacy—that is, public acceptance of a decision on the basis of the wisdom, necessity, or fairness of the governmental processes of allocating and then exercising choices. A wise manager must constantly keep these conditions in mind when dealing with controversial choices. The commission had thus left itself extremely vulnerable to a charge of usurping powers properly belonging to Congress, a charge that might enlist—or disarm—even those otherwise sympathetic to its consumer initiatives.

Thus the political context was nearly perfect for effective attacks designed to withdraw from the FTC the "loan" of responsibility for dealing with the problem of assuring that business practices were fair to consumers and competitors. Opponents would find this an ideal occasion to seek to restrict the authority and resources the FTC needed to carry out its mandate. As Pertschuk pressed ahead with the "kid-vid" proceedings, especially while announcing that a ban on advertising for children was a possibility, he ran a very grave risk that Congress would reverse the commission's actions.

In fact Congress eventually acted to prevent any "kid-vid" rule. It restricted the commission's current rule-making proceedings. It imposed a legislative veto on all future rules (a step later held unconstitutional by the Supreme Court). The FTC budget was slashed. The agency even had to be closed down for several days when angry conferees could not agree to authorize its continuing operation.

An Alternative Strategy

In retrospect it seems plain that radical changes in the political environment demanded a different strategy of exercising obvious restraint in rule-making and taking other steps to disarm the industry lobbyists who saw the time as ripe for stripping the commission of its most valued powers. Why then did the FTC continue with its dangerous strategy? Answering this question is a necessary preface to designing a better strategy with the aid of hindsight. For perhaps it was the fear of even worse consequences that dictated taking serious risks.

It is possible, of course, that people within the FTC were not sufficiently aware of the sweeping changes in sources of external support and opposition, becuase of weaknesses in the organization that reflected its unwavering commitment to a single path. Any organization, through its staff and structure, needs to be sensitive to changing conditions of outside support and needs internal incentives to bring these concerns into the discussion of prospective agency action. Some people within the FTC were sensitive to the developing assault on the agency and relatively sympathetic to the arguments being used in that assault. Pertschuk's organizational decisions made it more difficult for them to get a hearing and a reasonable response.

Another part of the answer is that some activities, like many of the new rules, were so fundamental to Pertschuk's hopes for the consumerist cause that he might well have pursued them at great political risk, even if he had seen very clearly the developing political changes. But there were three additional reasons why it was hard to change direction, all related to his own stakes in a position of leadership.

Pertschuk was appointed to lead the organization in consumer advocacy. That is what the president expected of him. That is what his history promised. That is why he took the job. Public managers have their own form of mandate, as difficult to reverse as the president's. They also have their own constituencies. Partschuk's political support came from consumer constituencies and members of Congress responsive to them and to consumer issues. Becoming merely the caretaker of an increasingly conservative Federal Trade Commission would threaten this support. Finally, a public manager needs the loyalty of his staff. Pertschuk's FTC was staffed with consumer advocates; it would have been costly to pull the reins on their enthusiasm.

One can say, perhaps too easily, that the task of the leader is to show supporters, staff, and those who appointed him that changing times require new strategies to advance their common cause. The alternative is that all go down together. But leading in a new direction requires opportunities for communication with, and persuasion of, the manager's friends and supporters. And it is very difficult to convey persuasively to true believers the new demands of changing times. The effort is always costly and almost always risky; a leader without followers is not a leader.

A manager chosen to lead consumer interests who becomes the voice of caution may lose the only support he has in a hostile environment.

Pertschuk had to address the ultimate issue of political leadership: how far one can move in new directions without breaking the bonds of loyalty of one's followers. If he abandoned "kid-vid," for example, representatives of consumer interests—the primary basis of his support—might doubt his dedication, steadfastness, and courage. Early retreat in the face of attacks in Congress would also show business interests that the commission was skittish and thus that its initiatives were vulnerable to a strategy based on vigorous lobbying. Reversal of his position on "kid-vid" would surely cause disarray among the commission staff, who knew this was his standard-bearing proposal for an organization dedicated to consumer advocacy.

The central problem, in short, was a familiar one in strategy: how to adjust the goals and activities of an agency to changed conditions of external support when, in the short run, the agency personnel persist in their beliefs, values, and habits. Here, however, the problem is compounded by the importance of not abandoning the manager's own lifetime commitments and of maintaining the trust of his personal and organizational constituencies. A well-chosen strategy for the FTC would have required not only actions designed to reduce the very substantial risk to the commission's rule-making powers but other actions designed to maintain the hope and commitment of the dedicated staff of the Federal Trade Commission and the loyalty to Pertschuk of both that staff and outside consumer groups.

One solution, perhaps the best, was later suggested by Pertschuk himself. He might have acknowledged that the most dramatic of the commission's rule-making initiatives, including particularly "kid-vid," were not appropriate for decision by the commission and referred them with some fanfare to the appropriate committees of Congress. There he and the commission could have appeared as vigorous advocates for even the most sweeping of measures without risking, by their advocacy, the powers of the commission. On the one hand, by avoiding an unpopular assertion of a questionable agency power, he would not have been gambling so recklessly with the resources of the commission in a game he was likely to lose. On the other hand, free to advocate strongly congressional restrictions, he would not have been publicly retreating from his convictions. His message to his supporters and staff would have been one of realism as to the location of needed political power, but not a personal or institutional compromise.

4 *Ends and Means*

I have argued that handling the politics of managing a government agency requires choosing goals that will elicit whatever external support their execution requires because of what the goals promise to do, or what they say about who and what are important, or what alliances they invite. The goals, moreover, must be within the capacity or the attainable capacity of the organization, or else the promises and statements will prove to be empty. But all of this talks to a relatively small fraction of the public—those particularly interested in the specific area the organization deals with. Another aspect of strategy speaks to a far wider public, informed by the press and broadcast media, whose interests are in the competence, fairness, and law-abidingness of government rather than in the direction taken by any particular organization. Surprisingly, this public is more interested in means than ends, in how whatever is done was accomplished rather than what goals were set.

An important part of the story of the Federal Trade Commission at the time Caspar Weinberger took over was the highly publicized charges of staggering incompetence and near corrupt partisanship. An important part of the story of the Federal Trade Commission at the time of Mike Pertschuk was the sense of overreaching as the commission stretched its statutory authority beyond what many thought were its legitimate limits. The organized interests of consumers (in the first case) and businesses (in the second) were no more important than their abilities to appeal to wider, relatively disinterested audiences by charges relating to *how* the agency was conducting its business.

Consider one particularly dramatic example. Anne Gorsuch's management problem at the Environmental Protection Agency was somewhat different from that facing either of the two chairmen of the FTC, though it was just as difficult as the one confronting Pertschuk. Weinberger had been expected to choose activities and to develop the FTC's capacity to meet the demands of those who thought his agency was doing far too little. Pertschuk was expected to cut back activities (without destroying the organization) to meet the demands of that sizable portion of the attentive public and the Congress that thought his agency was doing far too much. When Anne Gorsuch was appointed EPA administrator a month after President Reagan took office, she had still a third job: to reduce the commitment of resources and the level of regulatory activity in a program that had always had extremely strong popular support.

From the last Carter EPA budget (1981) to the proposed 1984 budget, EPA's total operating budget was cut by 22 percent. Its personnel levels were reduced by some 27 percent. These cuts—particularly severe in view of inflation—had been taken in ways that damaged the agency's long-term scientific capability at a time when its legislative mandate to deal with toxic substances and hazardous waste had increased significantly. These could hardly be popular steps, and the environmental interest groups organized to resist Gorsuch's efforts were powerful, as was the opposition in key positions in Congress. Yet her forced departure was as attributable to the *way* she handled her unpopular assignment as it was to *what* she did. She created the opportunity for opponents to make effective charges of incompetence, near corruption, and indifference to serious national problems.

Anne Gorsuch's twenty-two-month residence at EPA was riddled with controversy. From the outset, there were reports that she was meeting with a steady stream of industry representatives at the Interior Department; allegations that the Gorsuch team had a "hit list" of career employees to be fired or transferred; questions about her hiring of former lawyers, lobbyists, or consultants for industries heavily regulated by EPA; and an uproar over a mid-June reorganization of headquarters, which, among other things, abolished the enforcement office and farmed out most of its responsibilities to program offices. Critics said the last change would make EPA a toothless tiger in the enforcement area.

The key issue that ultimately brought down the Gorsuch regime was the

1980 law that established a $1.6 billion Superfund to clean up abandoned hazardous waste sites. Intensive congressional investigations and press exposés in late 1982 and early 1983 charged that Gorsuch and White House appointee Rita Lavelle, the head of the program, had engaged in "sweetheart deals" with industry, gross mismanagement practices, concerted efforts not to use Superfund money for fear that this would spawn "Son of Superfund" (more federal monies for cleanups), and connivance with White House personnel to announce (or not announce) Superfund cleanups on the basis of their effects on congressional races.

When Representative John Dingell's (D-Mich.) oversight subcommittee requested documents about specific Superfund cases in September 1982, the Justice Department instructed Gorsuch to send the relevant documents to Justice instead. Congressional committees then issued subpoenas requiring Gorsuch to appear with the documents. On November 30, the president, acting on the advice of his White House counsel and the attorney general, instructed Gorsuch not to comply with the subpoenas. The strategy quickly backfired: leaders of both parties in Congress bridled at the administration's action, and Dingell said publicly that leaked documents suggested political manipulation of a specific Superfund enforcement case. On December 16, with public interest in the confrontation rapidly mounting, the House, by a wide margin, voted Gorsuch in contempt of Congress. The Justice Department immediately filed suit in U.S. district court to halt the contempt proceedings.

Nature then intervened. At the end of 1982, freak floods led to a hazardous waste spillage (contamination from roads coated with dioxin) and the evacuation of homes in Times Beach, Missouri, spurring what one account labeled a "feeding frenzy" among the media. In short order the administration's suit was dismissed in court; Rita Lavelle was fired by Reagan (after she turned down a Gorsuch request to resign); fresh conflict of interest allegations were leveled against James Sanderson, a close Gorsuch adviser; old controversies, such as the one involving the "hit list," resurfaced; more top EPA employees resigned; and the White House brought in an interim management team of experienced officials in a last-ditch attempt to abate the crisis. On March 9, 1983, the President reluctantly accepted Gorsuch's resignation. ("She was doing a good job," Reagan later said, and "we, this administration, can be very proud of our record on the environment.")

Vulnerability to Public Attack

The wise manager of a government agency knows that his external support depends not only on views of the agency's goals and activities but also on the reactions of people who do not care much about what it is doing but see a relationship between its activities and some familiar weaknesses of government. Those who care greatly about what the agency is doing may themselves be relatively unconcerned about whether it is also an example of government waste or overreaching or partisanship or corruption or unresponsiveness or ineffectiveness. But the passionate partisans fighting for or against the agency and its programs see and recognize that these are the issues that will elicit the crucial, less self-interested support for their views of the sizable attentive public that is more broadly interested in the perennial American debate about the proper role of government.

At the heart of a manager's political concerns about the set of dangers associated with *how* activities are carried out is a simple, historical fact about opinion in America. For two centuries Americans have been remarkably ambivalent toward the activities and powers of executive agencies. The Bill of Rights reflects our historical fears of governmental overreaching into the lives of individuals. Watergate and the forced resignation of President Nixon showed the continuing power of this theme. From long before the time of President Jackson we have feared the effect of misplaced partisanship and, more serious, corruption. A pervasive suspicion that government is wasteful, inefficient, unresponsive to severe problems, and ineffective in handling those it addresses has as long a history. And yet, throughout the twentieth century, the size of government has increased immensely, creating a tension with abiding suspicions that has often been the touchstone of our politics, separating liberals from conservatives and those who emphasize the desirability of government responsiveness to citizen needs from those who are haunted by its historical problems.

Presidents and their challengers probe our fears and doubts about government in their search for votes. Along with prescriptions for the economy and national security concerns, attitudes toward these longstanding and widely shared suspicions about government have formed the dominant themes of presidential contests. Of course one candidate may point to a need for more government to handle pressing problems; another may urge less government so as to give individual initiative its head. But beyond this, incumbents may be attacked for widespread corruption, as President Truman was; or for overreaching, as President Nixon was; or for waste and inefficiency, as President Carter was; or for unresponsiveness, as President Reagan was.

The managers of government agencies often unwillingly provide the evidence to support these attacks on an administration. Thus, to protect both his own programs and the administration's survival, an agency manager must give special attention to any aspects of his organization's work that seem to confirm haunting, historical criticisms of executive government; for the press is likely to trumpet such agency failings to a wide audience interested in new evidence to support old prejudices.

The manager can find clues to these dangers in the history of his agency. Almost every program that enjoys the attention of a sizable public and of the media has, at any given time, its own particular vulnerability to popular attack as well as its own special claims to public support. Often the basis for invoking either opposition or support is merely anecdote, myth, prejudice, or surface impression; but, whatever the basis, public attitudes that will shape congressional response generally fall into familiar categories for each agency and program.

Waste and inefficiency constituted the highly predictable vulnerability of the former Department of Health, Education and Welfare (as has been true more recently of the Department of Defense); popular concern for the welfare of the needy, at least if their need was not their fault, was a well-established pillar of support for HEW. The Department of Justice is supported by belief in the overriding importance of law to our society and of that department to enforcement of the law; attacks on Justice typically focus on charges of partisanship, other bias, or governmental violations of individual rights. The Internal Revenue Service is supported by the understood need for public funds; it is threatened by attacks based on a widely held belief in the unfairness of many tax provisions and a latent public hostility to privacy-invading investigations.

The public that will read about, discuss, or debate such weaknesses of a particular program is likely to be broad enough to be important to the program's congressional supporters and opponents. And this attentive public will look for evidence and judge results in terms of categories that are or can be well-known in advance. A crucial part of developing a strategy for an organization is therefore for the manager to identify the agency's vulnerabilities to public attack and then to attend *both* to actions and events relating to these vulnerabilities (that is, to realities) *and* to public and congressional perceptions of such actions and events (that is, to appearances). The commissioner of internal revenue may not have to worry about public anger at estimates that taxpayers are evading paying 15 percent of the amounts owed as income tax. But in light of public hostility to welfare and "welfare cheats," the secretary of the Department of Health and Human Services must be greatly concerned about publication of a much smaller figure for fraud, waste, and abuse in his programs.

In short, the external support for an organization and its programs depends in important measure upon internal management. A manager can lose the support his organization needs not only by setting goals and engaging in activities that are not politically acceptable, as in the Pertschuk case, but also by failing—or *appearing* to fail—to accomplish what he has been charged with doing effectively and efficiently, without overreaching, corruption, or improper favoritism.

The Use of Public Suspicions of Government to Challenge an Organization's Leadership

The converse is also true; effective internal management depends upon external support: Congress and the White House must at least be willing to leave the manager with control over most important organizational decisions. That in turn depends upon his past success or failure in one crucial aspect of managing the organization he heads: his ability to deny opponents the opportunity to use his agency to confirm and exploit public suspicions about the vulnerabilities of government.

If the head of an organization appears to be an excellent manager, he will be left relatively free in his choice of means to carry out the organization's programs. He is likely to be entrusted with additional responsibilities and additional resources to carry them out. The price of appearing biased, indifferent, ineffective, or wasteful is more rigorous oversight, specific mandates from the legislature or superiors, and personal attacks that will undermine influence in the smoke of political battle. The programs will suffer, both directly by being denied resources or authority and indirectly through restrictions on the way available resources and authority can be used. Support for the manager by those who carry out the programs, or must cooperate in the execution of the programs, will diminish rapidly.

All of this is frequently played out in the context of a familiar contest for information between the legislature, which grants authority and resources, and the executive, which seeks, uses, and justifies the use of them. Oversight hearings are the historical field for this contest. "Leaks" have been the traditional source of needed "intelligence" for the legislature contemplating oversight, although more recently the creation of inspectors general within the large federal departments with responsibility to report to Congress has provided an additional source of information to start the game. The work of the inspector general of the Department of Defense under President Reagan provides a striking example.

The manager would prefer to be the only one who learns of failures or mistakes, so that he can take remedial action and not be held responsible for failures that he could not anticipate. Only in that way can he freely choose the remedy. He wants the agency to be judged not on its mistakes but on the way he and it handle the combination of trial, error, and correction—a far more tolerant setting. This depends upon his control, in the first instance, of information relevant to effectiveness, efficiency, fairness, legitimacy, and responsiveness.

To the legislature, the situation looks quite different. Managers hide failures and trumpet successes. It is the task of legislative oversight to see that agency activities are accomplished effectively, efficiently, and properly and to reconsider programs that cannot be administered in this way. That may require legislative action to restructure the management of the organization; it may require terminating or reducing a program. If the problem lies neither with the systems nor with the programs, it may require or justify attacks on the manager and steps to reduce his responsibility and authority.

From a legislative point of view, all this is very much the legitimate material of politics. Controversial programs and their managers are inevitably the subject matter of partisan politics in a democracy. They are the battleground of Democrats against Republicans, of liberals against conservatives. The battle is for public opinion, direction of government, and votes in elections. The very difficult context for management that it creates is much of the heat in the kitchen of government.

One final point deserves emphasis. Battles over the public's reaction to government agency and its programs, carried out by spirited political partisans in the daily press and in their periodic campaigns, occur in realm where appearances *are* political realities, where detailed justifications are impossible or ineffective, and where explanations may never catch up with accusations. It is very much the job of the manager of a government agency to attend to appearances whenever he is dealing with matters of agency vulnerability.

Weinberger's predecessor had allowed the FTC budget to show substantially more resources going to the labeling of textiles and furs than to antitrust enforcement at a time when the commission itself was reporting a massive increase in industrial concentration. In doing so, the former chairman was painting a target on himself and his agency. Chairman Pertschuk gave a champagne party to celebrate the initiation of the daring "kid-vid" rule making at a time when he was already under attack for abandoning neutrality between consumers and businesses and ignoring the limits of his powers. Neither the amount of money spent on furs and textiles nor the champagne party had much to do with important realities, but they were significant matters of appearance, relating to widely perceived agency vulnerabilities, and thus of central importance to the politics of management.

Appearances and Reality

When Joseph Califano became secretary of the Department of Health, Education and Welfare (HEW) in 1977 he immediately recognized the special vulnerabilities of his agency in terms of public attitudes toward government. The programs were expensive and had grown exceedingly rapidly. As the largest domestic agency, HEW was the most prominent target of criticism by those concerned about rapid governmental growth, a continuing budget deficit, and excessive taxation. Many of its programs, such as social security and medicare, had strong supporting constituencies; but for some of its largest undertakings—Aid To Families with Dependent Children (AFDC), medicaid, educational programs for the poor—the principal beneficiaries were the poor, who were unorganized and did not vote in significant numbers. A conservative tide was rising in the country and in the Congress. Inflation was serious, the economy was weak, the national budget was showing large deficits.

Some of HEW's major programs would obviously be the first to suffer if Congress or the president demanded large cuts in the federal budget. Others, like social security and medicare, which benefit large, organized voting constituencies, would be considerably safer. Without support from powerful constituencies and under attack because of their cost, the vulnerable programs of HEW could not afford to appear to be throwing money away. A dramatic showing of ineffectiveness or inefficiency can undermine support for even a relatively strong program. It can easily destroy a weak one.

Congress had already shown its willingness to intervene at HEW in the name of efficiency. In response to apparently lax efforts by Califano's predecessors to control waste, the Congress had created a statutory inspector general for HEW. The inspector general was charged with reporting regularly to Congress on problems and deficiencies in the department's programs, making recommendations for corrective action, and advising Congress what, if any, steps had been taken by the management of HEW to carry out those recommendations. The Congress had, in effect, partially reorganized the department to provide itself with detailed knowledge and concrete recommendations that could readily be made the basis of congressional action. With these, and on the further recommendations of its relevant committees, Congress could intervene intelligently and promptly in the management of HEW whenever it wished. A secretary of HEW was at some peril in ignoring the recommendations of his inspector general.

Vigorous action to control fraud and waste in HEW's programs clearly had to play a crucial part in Califano's strategy for the department. But one final fact is important to understanding the political problem at the core of this part of his strategy. There had been, was, and would continue to be billions of dollars of fraud, waste, and abuse in the HEW programs, whatever Califano did. In part this was simply a matter of arithmetic; even a small percentage of a budget of over $140 billion is a very large amount. More fundamentally, money was being distributed to millions of individuals who were likely to be no more honest than the average taxpayer and who were in far greater need. And at least for some of the largest and most sensitive programs, payments were handled by state and local officials working through a complicated organizational structure that gave them few incentives to scrutinize the payments carefully. In welfare, for example, states could benefit financially by using more federal funds to replace their own general relief funds; and it has proved extremely difficult to design an effective system for monitoring state payments.

Califano's strategic problem was to develop a plan for dealing with fraud and waste in HEW's programs that would be convincing and credible enough to blunt the arguments of program opponents and partisan political figures and that would be prompt and aggressive enough to maintain his own control of the issue. Yet no amount of effort could make the problem disappear quickly or even reduce its size to less than a few billion dollars, a figure of great potential usefulness to opponents. And Califano had to do these things while working with and through an inspector general who had been charged to report to Congress on problems, his recommendations for their solution, and what was done about his recommendations. That was a very difficult assignment.

Califano promptly initiated several dramatic new programs to detect fraud and waste and to make his own commitment very visible. At the same time he assigned the initial stages of a much more systematic approach to the problem to an extremely distinguished professional, Tom Morris, whom he had carefully selected as his first inspector general. The first systematic step they agreed upon was a comprehensive audit by the inspector general of the amount of fraud and waste in all of HEW's programs. This would provide a benchmark, an overall target for the managers of these programs. If there was any detail behind the estimates, it might provide more specific leads for their future efforts. The results would be furnished to Congress as part of the inspector general's first annual report. They could hardly be kept secret in any event. The figures would be motivating for managers of HEW programs even if they were made known only within the department. If they were made public as planned, there would be immense pressure for the managers to act quickly and forcefully to deal with the problem.

From the perspective of management without politics, of realities without appearances, this was an entirely sensible and admirably forceful first step. It certainly made sense from the point of view of HEW's first statutory inspector general. The position was created by Congress precisely to separate management from politics. Professional standards were to control, and Tom Morris represented the finest in professional standards of independent, scrupulously honest judgment, grounded in facts, systems, and auditing. He was the leading figure in a professionalized approach to problems of inefficiency at a time of increased skepticism about government programs. He wanted to see the new approach work and wanted to display the thoroughness, rigor, and independence that could build confidence in inspectors general. Morris had every reason to believe that Congress and Califano expected him to pursue the most complete and up-to-date appraisal of the facts and that this strategy would further the inspector general notion to which he was committed.

Morris was supposed to think about management in apolitical terms, but the manager of a highly visible governmental organization, such as Califano, has a quite different responsibility. When Califano sat down with Morris in the spring of 1977 and decided on an audit of all fraud and waste at HEW, he was addressing a matter of central strategic importance to the organization. Appearances can be as important as realities, and one could foresee that the published results of the audit would produce mammoth problems in maintaining external support because of the *appearances* of great inefficiency and misuse of government funds. The audit *did* have just those consequences, leading to editorial attacks on Califano and HEW; bringing spirited, widespread legislative assaults on his budget and powers; and finally allowing Ronald Reagan to denounce President Carter's failings on the basis of figures his own secretary of HEW had volunteered.

There was every reason to expect an honest estimate of fraud and waste in HEW's programs to be at least in the neighborhood of 5 percent. (In fact this was the figure Morris eventually arrived at.) Independent auditors in the private sector, using generally accepted accounting principles, regard that figure as the threshold for deciding whether an item bearing on income or expenditures is material and thus must be reported in public records. Waste and fraud at the Department of Defense were estimated to be higher and income tax evasion was assumed to be several times that much. More important, 5 percent of a budget for 1977 of $136 billion was close to $7 billion, a figure that is and sounds immense. To acknowledge that the department responsible for such unpopular programs as AFDC (welfare) was wasting more money than small states spent in a year would have frightening political implications for the department, its secretary, and even the president. Perhaps because they saw this, Califano's predecessors at HEW during the Ford administration had always found themselves unable to produce the estimates of total fraud and waste that their critics on the hill requested.

If he had focused on the political harm that might be done by such a report at the end of his first year, Califano would also have seen that there would be little he could do about it when the report had been prepared, let alone released. By then there would be little room to limit the damage to his goals. It should not and could not be suppressed. Califano could make clear that he ordered the report, but that message would be swamped by the dollar figure. He could try to emphasize how much of the figure was attributable to wasteful programs that Congress insisted on maintaining, but that would only deflect attention from the issue of a lack of management systems and skills to the weakness of HEW's programs. Neither message was acceptable. He could emphasize that most of the loss was waste rather than fraud, but how much difference would that make to the public or to hostile legislators?

There were, after all, only three alternatives. Either HEW was being badly managed *or* the programs were seriously deficient *or* the 5 percent figure, which could not realistically be the fault of an administration that had been in power for only a little over a year, was not so shocking. The last point, although true, could not be made persuasive. The others were equally damaging, although the first did more damage to the reputations of Califano and the people at HEW and the second to support for the programs themselves. The harm that was in fact done by the report could have been avoided only by more careful thought at an earlier date—before the report was produced.

Managing Appearances

The federal manager's primary responsibility in internal management is, of course, to worry about efficiency and effectiveness and their relationship to the success of important programs. This he shares with the inspector general. But the public manager has an additional responsibility: to consider the impact of steps of internal management—including the appearances they create and the political uses to which they can be put—on support for the organization and its programs. That a serious miscalculation in this realm was rare for Califano makes the particular instance all the more interesting.

If Congress had demanded this report with its damaging summary figure, Califano would have been obligated to produce it. If HEW prepared any such report, it would have to be honest, stating accurately the conclusions of the inspector general. But although Congress expected an annual report from the inspector general, it had not demanded any detailed summary of HEW's failings, and there was no adequate reason to volunteer it in Califano's first year in office. Situations may arise where legal or moral obligation requires the public manager to take steps that will undermine outside support for programs he regards as important or damage his own capacity to manage. To accomplish essential goals, it might even be necessary, under certain rare circumstances, to generate a firestorm of public opposition to the organization's practices. But where management objectives can be accomplished without inviting uninformed or partisan attacks, the manager's responsibility is to consider appearance and politics as well as reality and management and to do these things while telling the truth. All this would have been possible for Califano.

In either of two ways Califano could have accomplished his management purposes while avoiding misleading appearances. If he had requested an audit of fraud and waste in the HEW programs as they were in January 1977, when he and Morris took office, Califano could, early in his tenure, have produced useful figures and at the same time conveyed to a broad public that he was not responsible for the waste they revealed. Perhaps Califano expected this form of review; he may have been surprised that the inspector general instead prepared a more up-to-date audit. But Califano could not expect the inspector general to be responsible for the *politics* of managing and maintaining support for HEW's programs. That is the responsibility of the secretary. It is contrary to the very core of the concept of a professional, independent inspector general.

If Califano or the inspector general needed the more up-to-date audit for management purposes, this too could have been accomplished with far greater sensitivity to the political realities of fragile programs under vigorous attack at a time when they were unusually vulnerable, of partisan desire to make political capital of the failures of Secretary Califano and President Carter, and of growing public skepticism about government. Developing a preferred course of action is relatively straightforward.

Nothing required Califano or Morris to bring together a summary figure, of staggering proportions, in a single initial report to the Congress. Califano could have satisfied his need for an effective benchmark of fraud and waste in different programs by directing a sequential review of each major program separately. This would have been entirely consonant with Morris's sense of the professional responsibility of inspectors general.

They might have begun with medicare and social security, which produced two of the largest program losses in absolute terms (although smallest when stated as percentages of their program outlays). The resulting figures would not have threatened the programs—they were far too firmly supported by powerful, well-organized constituent groups. Califano and Morris could still have realized all the advantages of setting a benchmark and then taking steps to deal with fraud and waste against that background.

In addition, social security was a program that needed management attention but had successfully resisted the secretary's efforts to improve its processes. Encouraging some public support for those efforts, by releasing the audit figures for this program, could have helped.

Continuing a process of auditing each of the major programs in sequence, even if the figures were all made public, would probably have had much less serious consequences for HEW (and for President Carter when he ran against Ronald Reagan) than releasing a single overall estimate. The individual figures would have been less dramatic; steps to deal with the problems in each program could have been initiated and announced at the time the figures were released; public interest would have been likely to wane over time; and the final total would have been less newsworthy when it became available. The managerial benefits of the audit would, however, have remained; so would the demonstration of objective, professional competence by the newly established inspector general.

5 *Departmental Strategy and Presidential Stakes*

The strategy of a major federal department differs from that of a small agency like the Federal Trade Commission in three important ways. First, for a variety of reasons, more of its varied activities will remain constant despite changes in presidents and secretaries. Goals, I have emphasized, describe what it is hoped the organization's activities will do and produce; they say something about what and who is important; and they are the tokens out of which alliances are formed. For a major department with many goals, most of these functions are performed by choosing those relatively few areas in which activities are to be dramatically changed. Second, and related in an important way, a large department may be held together as much by certain institutionalized values as by shared activities. The stability or shifts in these values are an important part of strategy.

Finally, the president must rely on the department and the cabinet officer to carry out the promises he has made, to express concretely his themes about the role of government, and to show friendship to constituencies and legislators crucial to his political strength. I shall explore these issues in turn by contrasting the Department of Justice under Attorneys General Griffin Bell and Benjamin Civiletti during the Carter administration and under Attorneys General William French Smith and Edwin Meese during the Reagan administration.

The Department of Justice under Changing Administrations

If a visitor from Great Britain examined the Department of Justice in midterm during the Carter administration and then again in midterm during the Reagan administration, surely the most striking fact would be how much continuity there was. A great majority of attorneys were engaged in much the same activities, as were the tens of thousands of investigators, prison officials, and other nonattorneys under the attorney general.

A new attorney general knows that the Department of Justice must continue a very high proportion of its familiar activities. The same is true of any new department head. The activities have been authorized and funded over time by Congress, which has come to expect them; they have been accepted by a series of administrations; constituencies and expectations have developed around them; and the established responsibilities have become part of the fabric of governmental relationships with the private sector and among state and federal governmental units. Attorney General Smith did not contemplate any major changes in the way the Civil Division handled its defense of routine suits against the United States or in the way other attorneys handled the process of taking private property, with compensation, for governmental purposes.

What does characterize a new attorney general's tenure are the areas in which he makes changes in familiar activities or takes on new directions or aborts initiatives of his immediate predecessor. These decisions define his goals. The people they favor will come to be seen as the department's new constituencies. The symbolism of these decisions will be gratifying to some and threatening to others. With all these consequences, the new directions set by an incoming cabinet secretary may be the result of his own choice, or dictated by presidential needs, beliefs, and politics, or mandated by Congress.

The changes an outside observer would have noted at Justice were all chosen by the administration itself. Nothing an administration does in the area of law has more important or permanent effects than the appointment of judges. The Carter administration had reached out, in a wholly unprecedented way, to appoint women and minorities to the federal bench. Implicit in that decision was a notion that the judges' backgrounds have considerable influence on their decisions and that the law in the United States should reflect the life experience of women and minorities. The Reagan administration moved sharply in a very different direction: the appointment as judges (and as justices of the Supreme Court) of lawyers with a very conservative view of the role of courts and with no wish to see the courts as activist champions of minorities, the poor, and the politically powerless. President Reagan's choices would be far more deferential to tradition, established values, and the role of elected political institutions.

The Carter administration had emphasized the need to investigate and prosecute corrupt, fraudulent, and reckless actions of established centers of wealth and power as well as directing law enforcement at its traditiona federal targets such as organized crime and narcotics dealers. It considered violent street crime the responsibility of local government. Under the Reagan administration white-collar crime was pursued initially with less personnel and less visible concern. Reagan's men had far less concern about the dangers of social inequality in choosing the focus of law enforce ment. The Reagan administration repeatedly declared its emphasis on violent crimes; but by way of action in this area of traditionally local responsibility it could offer only greater attention to narcotics trafficking attacks on judicial decisions protecting suspects against police, and meet ings to "coordinate" with local authorities.

Still feeling the effects of Watergate, the Carter administration gave the Department of Justice an important role in controlling the activities of the Central Intelligence Agency and the Federal Bureau of Investigation. At torneys General Smith and Meese reversed this direction, focusing on the costs to crime control and internal security of an excessive concern about civil liberties. The Carter administration had supported the Supreme Cour in some of its most politically controversial decisions or at worst main tained a position of neutrality. The Department of Justice under Presiden Reagan let it be known that it, like the Moral Majority, wanted a reversal o decisions forbidding prayer in school, establishing remedial affirmativ action programs, and protecting a woman's right to choose whether to hav an abortion.

Smith and Meese sought the most basic changes in direction in two area of substantial constituent and public interest: antitrust and civil rights More tolerant of concentrations of industrial wealth and power than it predecessor had been, the Smith team announced that it was relaxing th requirements for mergers, and it settled major antitrust cases against tw corporate giants, AT&T and IBM. Most prior administrations had viewe with suspicion mergers of giant corporations, reflecting amorphous b long-established public fears of huge accumulations of capital in the con trol of a relatively few individuals. The Reagan administration abandone this posture as a matter of economic and social philosophy and in respons to the growing importance of international trade. It also sought to reduc the incentive that the prospect of triple damages gave to private parties t sue for antitrust violations; and it wanted to allow manufacturers to fix th price at which their goods could be sold by retailers. The department's emphasis in enforcement was on the core abuse in antitrust laws—price fixing. The activities of major industries were to be less subject to challenge by the government or private parties.

Finally, the most dramatic and public changes in direction came in the area of the civil rights of blacks, Hispanics, and women. Emphasizing a century of discrimination and disadvantage, the Carter administration (and its Republican predecessors) had supported congressional and judicial efforts to remedy the effects of historic unfairness to racial and ethnic minorities, particularly blacks. Never popular, court-ordered busing was still regarded by the Carter administration as a sometimes necessary remedy for school desegregation. The Civil Rights Division under Attorneys General Smith and Meese made every effort to prevent the transportation of pupils to schools outside their neighborhoods. The Justice Department set itself against court desegregation decrees that involved busing in any form.

The Carter administration and its predecessors had recognized a role for quotas or targets to achieve affirmative action as a remedy for traditional discrimination against minorities in employment. The Reagan administration regularly and forcefully opposed any form of minority preference in hiring, promotion, or retention. And, last, in a variety of ways the Reagan administration reduced the department's commitment to improving the position of women.

Throughout the civil rights area the central policy of the Reagan administration was color-blind, sex-blind neutrality and a halt to most forms of affirmative action. It denounced both social policy and judicial decisions formed in light of the disadvantages of the "average" member of a group that had long been the victim of discrimination. In the view of the Reagan people, only individuals who had personally suffered and proved personal victimization by discrimination deserved some form of remedy.

The Multiple Goals of a Governmental Conglomerate

Against this background it is worth reviewing what strategy means for an agency as large as the Department of Justice or even Health and Human Services (HHS). Obviously part of the strategy is to respect many of the expectations that have been made part of the responsibilities of the particular department over the years. A major department is necessarily part of a system of relationships and allocated responsibilities from which it cannot withdraw without major dislocations and immense political repercussions. New goals and changed activities are developed against this backdrop.

Because the department's responsibilities—inherited and newly chosen—are often extremely varied, its strategy may have to be expressed in terms of a *set* of goals (rather than a single goal), appealing to very different constituencies and to different concerns in the Congress. Still, much of what I have said about a strategy for the Federal Trade Commission applies, with some modification, to an organization like the Department of Justice.

Its leaders must develop or embrace a set of goals and activities that have the same three characteristics that Caspar Weinberger sought at the Federal Trade Commission. First, the goals and activities must further the objectives of the agency's leaders (including, as we shall see, the president). Second, the agency's activities must garner enough outside support to assure that they are funded, granted adequate authority, and sustained when challenged in courts or Congress and that they develop a legitimacy that avoids prolonged conflict with other powerful actors. Third, the organization must be able and willing to carry out the chosen activities and goals; or steps must be taken to change the organization so that it can and will support the new goals and activities. The second and third requirements are closely related. Objectives that are opposed internally will more readily find opposition in Congress, the media, and constituency groups. Outside opposition will strengthen internal dissent too. And, as we saw in the last chapter, persistent failures to carry out goals efficiently and fairly will undermine external support.

We have already seen that there is an additional and very central requirement for the goals and activities of an executive department. They must be consistent with and supportive of the president's objectives, themes, and political needs. It may be wise policy for a president to separate much of his political needs from the operations of the Department of Justice, as President Carter decided to do. But even that decision is generally made as much on the basis of the political wisdom of respecting and emphasizing the independence of the Department of Justice as it is on the inherent desirability of that result. The president's broad objectives and needs must inform the agency manager's choice of goals and strategy; democratic accountability demands no less. The far more extensive institutional knowledge of the appointed manager may dictate that he play the integrating organizing role in choosing a strategy with the president, but he plays this role subject to a central obligation to honor the president's goals and themes.

Finally, for a large and multifaceted department like the Department of Justice there are synergistic effects among activities. Thus there is more to the choice of a strategy than the discrete calculations of whether each activity individually generates the external support and organizational acceptance it needs. A mix of goals and activities may include some that are unpopular (for example, legal actions against overcrowded state prisons) along with others (for example, investigations and prosecutions of narcotics dealers) popular enough to maintain overall public, congressional, and staff support for the organization. Similarly, some activities may be undertaken now with the understanding that others, to be begun later, will prevent the development of any too threatening opposition. Activities may be chosen because they can be handled conveniently and inexpensively by the same people or processes or with the same skills, training, or information as are already committed to the organization's other activities. Seeing political and practical connections between the various goals and activities of a multifaceted organization is part of constructing its strategy.

All of this assumes that a major department is like a loosely structured conglomerate corporation—a collection of goals and activities related to each other only in the administrative convenience or the pattern of political opportunities provided by joint handling. In these limited terms the changes in the Department of Justice under Attorneys General Smith and Meese represented a mere shift in the sources of congressional and constituency support and a change in the pattern of benefits provided and symbols embraced—matters with which special interest groups and larger publics identify.

A liberal House Judiciary Committee could be expected to resist the loosening of restraints on the CIA or FBI under the Reagan administration; a far more conservative Senate Judiciary Committee would be more sympathetic. Supporters of "law and order" would applaud the attention to crime in the streets. Senate liberals and a wide political spectrum of the press would condemn the appearance of indifference to crime in executive suites. Small businesses would be opposed to the change in direction of antitrust activity; large corporations and unions might be supportive. Opponents of affirmative action would applaud steps taken in the Civil Rights Division. Blacks and hispanics would feel abandoned after nearly twenty years of steadfast support by the Department of Justice. Supporters of women's rights would be angry; the Moral Majority, appreciative. These are the changes that one would expect with a change in administration. They affect both the nature and the extent of the Department of Justice's support in ways that are more complicated than, but fundamentally similar to, what we have seen in the cases involving the Federal Trade Commission.

Strategy and Institutionalized Values

But there is more to the strategy of a major department. A major department is not simply a conglomerate. It frequently has been allocated a particular role—and is expected to demand consideration of particular values—in the policy debates and decision processes taking place among governmental departments and among the executive branch, the courts, the Congress, and state governmental units. Organizational power—the department's influence in bureaucratic and legislative struggles—takes on form and has weight in terms of the role that has been assigned and the values entrusted to the department. The strength of its operating capabilities also depends on the staff's understanding of what is important and right in terms of that role and the values it expresses.

The special powers committed to the Department of Justice in matters of governmental choice have derived from the importance of respect for law, *as interpreted by the courts,* in every aspect of federal policy. The special role of the department has been to construe and enforce the law and to act as intermediary between the courts (as the ultimate high priests of the only established American religion: law) and the executive branch. In contrast, the influence of HHS and its predecessor, HEW, depended upon the agency's special capabilities and complicated responsibilities in handling vast support and research programs for the needy, helpless, and ill and upon its important funding relationships to states, cities, providers of social and medical services, and interest groups representing beneficiaries. Dramatically different, the authority of the Department of Justice in government councils is as the final interpreter, short of the courts, of what the law permits and requires. Nothing shows this more clearly than the limits that are placed upon even a president by a formal opinion of the attorney general saying that a particular course of action would not be legal.

The attorney general has generally been less of an advocate of administration policies than other cabinet secretaries. His loyalty to the president has had to be shared with his loyalty to the attributes of law: scrupulous fairness, equality, and concern about the neutrality and regularity with which governmental powers are exercised. The attorney general and the Department of Justice are expected to share the qualities of the Supreme Court. The department and the attorney general may serve the president, but both derive the public support they can bring to a president from the notion that they maintain a prior obligation to the law and that, like judges—indeed assisting judges—they represent the commands of the law within and outside government circles.

Attorney General Bell describes this broad theme of his strategy for the Department of Justice during his tenure under President Carter in his opening discussion from *Taking Care of the Law,* which he wrote with Ronald Ostrow. He refers to a letter he wrote the president reminding him that he had ''directed me to establish an independent Department of Justice, a neutral zone in the government, where decisions will be made on the merits free of political interference or influence.'' He notes that ''the administration's views on matters of law, then, were to be decided at the Justice Department, not at 1600 Pennsylvania Avenue.''* Bell recognized that he could be overruled by the president and fired, but until that happened his responsibility for furnishing independent legal advice and judgment remained, as did the president's responsibility to respect that independence of judgment.

Bell uses three examples to describe the working out of that strategy—the constant struggle for departmental independence in matters of law and the challenge to that independence posed by the policy views of the president's staff. In each case his battle was to support the views of an assistant attorney general who had carefully considered the law and the facts. In one case the assistant attorney general in charge of the Office of Legal Counsel had ruled that the first amendment forbade certain federal employment training funds (CETA) being used in church schools in particular ways. Catholic constituencies were seriously concerned and the president was pursuaded to overrule the Department of Justice, a step Bell described as ''extraordinary'' and led him to consider resigning. In another case the solicitor general and the assistant attorney general for civil rights devel-

*Griffin B. Bell with Ronald J. Ostrow, *Taking Care of the Law* (New York: William Morrow and Co., 1982).

oped a position on whether a white applicant could object to quotas established for minorities in medical school admissions at a state university. No issue could be more public, more fraught with political ramifications, and more inflammatory. Yet Bell argues that it was one of law, in which the Department of Justice needed substantial independence. Finally, Bell discusses the president's personal efforts to secure federal prosecution of a police officer who had wantonly slain a Mexican-American youth and whose prosecution in Texas had resulted in only a five-year sentence. The discussion makes it clear that Bell believed the president was not giving appropriate respect to departmental views and policies affecting legal judgments and processes (policies about reprosecution of someone already convicted in a state court).

Bell's claim for departmental independence rests on the Department of Justice's responsibility to take guidance from the law, and thus from the courts that authoritatively interpret the law, as well as from the president. In asserting his independence from White House policy on some broad classes of matters, at least unless the president is prepared to take the "extraordinary" step of intervening, the attorney general is necessarily saying that he and the Department of Justice are not simply advocates when they decide whether government funds can be used in parochial schools, or whether white applicants can object to a state school's quota that benefits minorities, or whether five years is a long enough sentence by a state court to prevent the federal government from retrying a police officer for the very same murder. A private lawyer would feel comfortable in representing either side of any of these controversies. As attorney general, Bell felt that he had sterner obligations and narrower limits, reflecting his responsibility to decide what the law commands or permits and the administration's responsibility to follow that guidance without waiting for a court to order it into compliance.

The attorney general's independence and his power in government councils also depend upon the special relationship of the Department of Justice to the courts. Ultimately, the courts resolve what the law requires and permits in the United States. The attorney general cannot plausibly claim independence from presidential politics or policy in the name of some view of the law inconsistent with that adopted by the courts. His influence with other agencies and with private individuals deeply committed to the stability and order that law has given the United States depends upon his role as an interpreter and enforcer of what the courts declare to be the law. In these conflicting obligations—to the president and the courts, to politics and law—is rooted the independence that Attorney General Bell demanded.

Attorney General William French Smith and his successor, Edwin Meese, profoundly changed the strategy of the Department of Justice when they determined to set the department on the path of advocacy of the president's policy views even when these were opposed to the firmly-arrived-at decisions of the courts and when they decided to use the position of the attorney general to attack the way courts had been handling their responsibilities. In October 1981, for example, Smith delivered a major policy speech before the Federal Legal Council in which he outlined his agenda for his tenure. "In recent decades," he explained, "at the behest of private litigants and even the executive branch itself, federal courts have engaged in a similar kind of judicial policy-making [similar to the judicial opposition to the New Deal in the 1930s]. In the future, the Justice Department will focus upon the doctrines that have led to the courts' activism. We will attempt to reverse this unhealthy flow of power from state and federal legislatures to federal courts—and the concomitant flow of power from state and local governments to the federal level."

In the summer and fall of 1985, Attorney General Meese delivered several major addresses on the same theme. In the fall of 1986 he took the occasion of a major address to argue that Supreme Court decisions do not have the force of law, except to the parties to the particular case. Any such attacks on the courts are necessarily expressions of presidential policy, not of the competing demands of law as authoritatively interpreted by the very courts being challenged. An administration can properly attack the drift of Supreme Court decisions. But when the attorney general takes the lead in doing so and adopts too exclusively the administration's views of what the law should be, he is fundamentally shifting the department's strategy. He is forfeiting much of the department's claim to independence from the White House and to a controlling position in determining the lawfulness of executive action or the validity of the claims of the executive in a conflict with Congress. He is gaining, instead, the authority and rewards of loyalty to the president and his constituencies.

An overriding and single-minded dedication to the job of advocate for the president wherever his views or interests are implicated, without pretense of a competing responsibility to the courts and to the law *as they have interpreted it,* is a defensible notion of the role of the Department of

Justice. But giving such plain priority to the role of advocate, with its close ties to the politics of presidential constituencies and its dependence upon the themes of national campaigns, is a very different course from that Attorney General Bell and Attorney General Civiletti were trying to steer. The two roles emerge from different strategies, draw support to the department from different sources, and convey quite different messages to the staff of the department.

Strategy and Presidential Goals, Themes, and Political Needs

There is a final special aspect of a departmental strategy, perhaps the most interesting. Because the president's themes and policies and the demands of his political constituencies must be played out largely at the departmental level, the cabinet secretary has special obligations to the president. At the same time, the articulated concerns of the president represent an opportunity for the agency head. Through the declaration of his themes and goals, the president promises support from all others subject to his authority or respectful of his bargaining influence for activities designed to further those goals or themes. To the department head, the president's expressed concerns are a letter of credit usable to support a range of activities thought desirable by the cabinet secretary, so long as these also obviously further the chosen policies and constituencies of the president.

In the aftermath of Watergate, President Carter made a major campaign theme of integrity in government and, more specifically, the independence of the Department of Justice. Black and hispanic constituencies were important to his electoral base; the advancement of civil rights, and particularly the broadening of the background of judges to include minorities and women, were major policies. His attorneys general, Griffin Bell and Benjamin Civiletti, had to make these themes, policies, and constituencies part of their plans for the department. They established new rules forbidding contact from the White House or the hill with anyone immediately responsible for a criminal prosecution, restricting contact to the attorney general and deputy attorney general. They gave the assistant attorney general and the U.S. attorneys close to absolute independence in the making of prosecutorial decisions. As we have seen, they gave great weight to the views of their staff on questions of law, even to the point of considering resignation when the White House "interfered." They pressed vigorously in the area of civil rights, following the path of their Democratic predecessors of the 1960s, who had made the vast expansion of minority rights and voting powers fundamental goals of their administrations.

As candidate and president, Reagan did not question the broadly accepted theme of equality in its core form of prohibitions against intentional discrimination on the ground of race. But he eschewed policies intended to increase the shares of power, status, or wealth enjoyed by minorities and women. To the contrary, his campaign promised an end to affirmative action, a focus on the individual rather than the minority group, and a new solicitude for the interests of those who felt they had been ignored by liberals for too long. Other major campaign themes involved halting excessive government interference in economic life and upholding traditional values including school prayer and a prohibition of abortion, values embraced by religious fundamentalists as well as other constituencies. Reagan promised to end coddling of criminals and give new respect to the police and military who protect ordinary citizens from enemies in the streets or abroad.

These themes, policies, and constituencies had to be recognized by Attorneys General Smith and Meese. As we have seen, they directed or encouraged sharp changes in the department's civil rights and antitrust enforcement policies. There was new litigating and legislative support for the representatives of "traditional" social values who felt threatened by the weakening of a conventional moral fabric. Judges were appointed to represent such traditional virtues, not neglected constituencies. The attorney general set up a commission on violent crime, although the federal government can do little in this area, and the newly elected president quickly pardoned the top-level FBI officials prosecuted by his predecessors for ignoring the constitutional rights of Americans in the pursuit of violent dissenters against the war in Vietnam.

The fact that presidential themes, policies, and constituencies must be considered by the cabinet secretary is hardly surprising. But what does this mean in practice? The president and his staff know what they want to deliver and express, but they cannot tell what the costs of furthering the president's goals will be in a particular case and how their wishes relate to other aspects of the strategy for the department. Consider the latter first.

President Carter was personally outraged when he saw pictures of the Mexican-American boy wantonly killed by a police officer in Texas. Honoring and protecting civil rights was also a major policy of his administration and theme of his campaign. The Mexican-American population in Texas could be of great importance to his prospects in a major state when he would run for reelection. On these bases he felt free to hint broadly that the Department of Justice would reconsider its decision not to retry in federal court the police officer who had already been convicted for the slaying in state court and sentenced to five years in prison.

President Carter and his staff could not, however, decide what weight to give a long-established policy of the Department of Justice for relating its efforts to that of state prosecutors. The policy, which had become part of the department's strategy, allowed multiple prosecutions for the same conduct only in exceptional circumstances. Moreover, applying long-established department policies consistently, despite the contrary wishes of elected officials, even the president, was necessary if the attorney general was to maintain another element in the department strategy *and* a major theme of the president—the nonpartisan, professional independence of the department. Deputy Attorney General Civiletti and Attorney General Bell refused to direct a second prosecution of the police officer. The president, to his credit, accepted that conclusion despite his personal disagreement. Only the attorney general and his people in Justice could decide how to relate the competing considerations. The president was prepared to accept the attorney general's centrality in making that decision.

A few years later Attorney General Smith and, more directly, Deputy Attorney General Edward Schmvlts faced another problem in integrating presidential themes, policies, and constituencies with a strategy for the Department of Justice. In 1970 the Internal Revenue Service had ruled that racially segregated private schools are not entitled to a tax exemption and that donors to such schools are not entitled to tax deductions for their contributions. This ruling had been litigated in two courts of appeals, both of which had affirmed the IRS position. Threatened by these rulings, schools run by fundamentalist religious groups in the South raised the issue still again, appealing to the United States Supreme Court as well as to friendly representatives in Congress, including Republican Congressman Trent Lott. They wanted the Department of Justice to reverse the position it had held for over a decade and invite the Supreme Court to rule that the Internal Revenue Service had exceeded the law in denying tax benefits on the ground that a private school discriminated against blacks.

As a candidate, President Reagan had made his position on this particular issue clear. He said he opposed "the IRS's attempt to remove the tax exempt status of private schools by administrative fiat," and the 1980 Republican platform promised to "halt the unconstitutional vendetta launched by Mr. Carter's [sic] IRS Commissioner against independent schools." The president had also very recently noted, in reviewing a summary of his mail, which included a letter on this issue from Congressman Lott, that he favored intervening in the Supreme Court case on behalf of the religious schools.

Deputy Attorney General Schmults confronted two opposing interpretations of the law. One camp, prominently represented by the head of his Civil Rights Division, Brad Reynolds, argued from original intent that nothing in the language or history of the Internal Revenue Code granted the powers the Internal Revenue Service had asserted in 1970. The other camp, represented by the acting solicitor general, Larry Wallace, and the commissioner of internal revenue, Roscoe Egger, argued from a more flexible view of legal sources that what had happened since 1970, including a number of court decisions and several actions by Congress indicating acceptance of the IRS position, made clear the power of the IRS to deny tax exemption to segregating schools. One could adopt either a fundamentalist or a more modern view of how law was made. As we have seen, on this issue the attorney general had stated his position firmly, declaring that the Justice Department would henceforth "attempt to reverse [the] unhealthy flow of power from state and federal legislatures to federal courts."

It was quite clear, however, that the administration would find it difficult—in all likelihood impossible—to convince the Supreme Court to overrule a decade of executive policy accepted by the Congress on several occasions and affirmed by several courts of appeals. But unlike its predecessors, the Reagan administration Department of Justice did not feel obligated to limit its litigating positions to those it felt the courts were likely to accept. It did not see itself as an independent entity somewhere *between* the president and the courts. It generally stood far more firmly on the side of the president.

Schmults and Smith, after consulting Secretary of the Treasury Donald Regan and his deputy, decided to overrule Wallace and Egger, to alter a longstanding executive position, and to support the president's campaign statements, constituencies, and policies by asking the Supreme Court to declare all that had happened since 1970 unlawful and to order the granting of tax exemptions and deductions to segregated schools and their donors.

The result was a disaster. The Supreme Court, in an 8–1 vote, rejected the narrow view of IRS powers that Smith and Schmults had sought to advance. The segregated schools were denied their exemption. Moreover, the department left the president looking like a supporter of segregation, a posture he most definitely did not want to assume. Consequently he felt it necessary to offend his conservative allies by pronouncing his firm opposition to the policies of these schools and proposing legislation denying them tax exemptions. The entire episode was costly in terms of Republican electoral support; in addition, the Department of Justice was weakened in both external support and internal cohesion. There are lessons to be learned from that set of events.

Addressing the Question in Terms of Presidential Stakes

The first and simplest lesson to be learned from the case of the segregated schools is that an executive department's actions and strategies must reflect real presidential interests, not the fleeting reactions of a very busy incumbent or his staff. Identifying where the president's interests really lie in a complicated world of shared powers and presidential politics requires hard thought, not just "touching base" with the White House.

Most decisions made by the attorney general or any other political appointee cannot be made by the president or the White House staff. Most do not involve important policy or electoral stakes for the president and thus should be decided as a matter of broad organizational strategy in light of the goals chosen by those appointed by the president, albeit with a recognition of the occasions on which they are borrowing against the president's credit with Congress, particular constituencies, or the public at large—or adding to that credit balance. In choosing those broad goals and arriving at that strategy the appointed manager will, of course, already have given great weight to the objectives, themes, and political needs of the president.

Even in decisions that *do* involve the president's electoral needs or fundamental policies in an important way, that consideration should not always override the goals chosen by the organization's leaders, although it must be taken very seriously. No president in recent years has demanded more consideration of his views and of his constituencies than has President Reagan. Surely the attorney general, the secretary of the treasury, and their deputies were trying to do the president's bidding when they overruled the acting solicitor general and the commissioner of internal revenue.

But in doing so, they did a very poor job of serving the president. He needed judgment as much as he needed loyalty from them.

The politics of the president's position on the issue of segregated schools should have been clear. He wanted to grant a tax exemption to the schools. He wanted a policy of hostility toward judicial activism. But, *plainly overriding both these considerations,* he did not want to appear personally to favor racial segregation. There was only one way to combine these three positions: by a powerful and broadly persuasive argument that the law, properly interpreted, denied the Internal Revenue Service the powers it had asserted for more than a dozen years. The president had to be seen as doing no more than obeying the law, the most fundamental obligation of every administration.

The matter was as simple as this. If the most respected lawyers and legal scholars overwhelmingly rejected the Reagan administration's interpretation of the law or if, much worse from the administration's point of view, the Supreme Court sharply repudiated that position, then the president would be left with only the policy of favoring the freedom of schools to segregate (or, worse, segregation itself) as an explanation for his position. Broad segments of the public would take from the Court (and not from administration spokesmen) their cues as to whether the law was forcing Reagan to do what he would not himself choose. At a minimum, the crucial political question was whether the administration's position would be received with some sympathy by a solid minority of the Supreme Court. If not, the president would be profoundly embarrassed personally and politically and the attorney general would be set back in his efforts to restrain the courts.

No one seems to have made the Supreme Court's likely decision a central question. Certainly there was reason for concern. Every sign pointed to repudiation of the department's position. One of the attorney general's primary purposes was to constrain the Court and repudiate its conception of its own powers. The Supreme Court would not share *that* purpose. No policy was more firmly the creation of the Supreme Court than desegregation. The administration's argument would be that, although it favored desegregation, it wanted the Court to say that the executive branch lacked the power, which Congress had for a decade assumed it had, to further this policy. The Supreme Court would not quickly accept responsibility for thwarting the wishes of both the legislative and executive branches on a matter so deeply at the heart of its own historic concerns.

The administration's argument would depend upon its fear that, if the Court recognized this special place for policies against discrimination, it might then go wild in other areas, a fear the Court would hardly share. All this was to occur in a context of review of tax regulations, where the Court had traditionally given great deference to the views of the Internal Revenue Service. Obviously there was a very strong chance that the Supreme Court would refuse this invitation to repudiate its own policies, leaving the president standing without the fig leaf of legality to cover a result favoring racist policies.

There was an alternative but hardly more promising route. The Internal Revenue Service could be ordered to revoke its regulation and grant exemptions to segregated schools. But, as a matter of political realities, that action would have to be defended on the ground that it was required as a matter of law, despite a dozen years of contrary interpretation by Congress, the executive branch, and the courts. To revoke the regulation as a simple matter of policy would be to announce the wholly unacceptable: that the administration favored assistance to segregation. And it would not be plausible to reverse the IRS position as a matter of law without giving the Supreme Court, the body almost all citizens believe speaks finally on such matters, the opportunity to address the issue already before it. Changing the administration's position administratively might, in short, avoid the risk of a Supreme Court repudiation—but only at the cost of appearing to favor assisting segregated schools and to fear submitting the issue to the Supreme Court. The fig leaf of the requirements of legality would be too small.

Finally, if there was any hope that no one might notice how small the fig leaf was, that hope was dashed by the positions of Larry Wallace, the acting solicitor general, and Roscoe Egger, the commissioner of internal revenue. The commissioner commands the respect and loyalty of tax lawyers throughout the country, who rely on his stalwartness on matters of law and principle to prevent administrative overreaching in revenue collection. The solicitor general's office has enjoyed a tradition of respect for its position in constitutional adjudication that no attorney general and no administration has fully shared, because that office is expected to place loyalty to the law and the Court on a par with its responsibility to the administration in power. To order the acting solicitor general to repudiate his views of the Constitution and the commissioner of internal revenue to repudiate his views of the Internal Revenue Code was to invite the widespread opposition of the bar, joined in this case by all those concerned about civil rights. The Supreme Court depends upon the solicitor general to support its views in the councils of the executive branch. To order that office to reverse its position would remind the Court of the important stake it has in the independence of the solicitor general.

It is easy enough to see what question Smith and Schmults should have asked and what the answer would have been. The question is whether the department had a sufficient chance of advancing the attorney general's notion of the relation of courts and agencies to Congress in this particular case (and of redeeming the president's campaign promises) to outweigh the chance that the administration would be widely perceived as supporting assistance to segregation as a matter of policy rather than in response to the commands of the law.

In fact, the gains to be made were small; the possible losses were immense. The chance of obtaining the gains was small; the risk of losing was great. The decision was indefensible as a matter of politics and presidential stakes. It was also implausible as an occasion for trying to advance the attorney general's notions of the role of the courts, for these notions were far more likely to be set back than advanced.

In sum, a president must come to agreement with the heads of his departments on the broad agency goals and strategy that can reconcile the core values and purposes of the department with his own presidential themes and policies. Once the broad outlines of such a strategy are in place, its application to specific situations apparently implicating presidential objectives, themes, or political needs is primarily a responsibility of the appointed manager. The department head knows more about the situations in which his agency acts, the nature of its activities, the capabilities and inclinations of his staff, and the views of other powerful interested parties. The president wants decisions consistent with *both* his policies and interests *and* longer-term, broader-based departmental strategies. He needs a strategy that incorporates his broad themes and objectives and he also needs decisions that integrate his more particular concerns with the broader strategy. He can, as we have often seen, be undone by swift, unquestioning obedience.

6 *Sources of Legitimacy*

Still another dimension of managerial strategy merits serious attention. A manager needs to have even unpopular decisions accepted, and he needs acceptance of other decisions even by those who disagree with his judgments. In both cases acceptance of the decision often depends upon acceptance of a political theory that legitimates choice by a particular official or institution or by a particular process or in terms of some accepted standard. Acceptance of the manager's decision often depends upon its "legitimacy"—a recognition that the manager was the right person to make that decision and that at least the grounds or basis and the method of analysis used for the choice were proper.

There are three great currents of legitimacy. A manager's unpopular decision may be accepted because it is an expression of the views and priorities of the president and of the democratic mandate delivered by the people in electing him. A manager's decision may, alternatively, be accepted because it is simply an interpretation of what the law or Congress required, because it represents the application of an expert judgment to what is simply a factual question (there being no dispute about the underlying value judgments that made the factual question relevant), or because it reflects that complicated mixture of fact, expertness, and values that constitutes a professional judgment about medicine, law, science, accounting, military strategy, or architecture. In each of these situations the acceptance depends upon the relationship of the decision to unquestioned normative notions of what process, sense of relevance, and style of thought are to be expected from those charged with making such decisions. Finally, even an unpopular decision may be accepted as the type of compromise that is necessary when the Congress and the president disagree in a particular area.

A manager's approach to legitimacy shapes every aspect of an agency's strategy, from external support to the deeply held values of the staff. Above all, it determines the alliances to which the manager can turn. Several issues warrant attention. First, it is important to show the sweeping impact of a choice among the three possible roles: advocate of the president's positions; nonpolitical expert, professional, or quasi-judge; and mediator between the executive and the legislative (or judicial) branches. Second, there is the question who makes this choice and who must accept it. What are the relationships among the manager, his executive branch superiors including the president, and the Congress? Finally, it is important to consider the relationship between sources of legitimacy and the nature of particular issues, for not all issues can be handled in each of the three ways.

The Importance of the Choice

Two examples will illustrate the importance of the basis on which legitimacy is claimed. The first involves a choice between seeking legitimacy in a quasi-judicial role and seeking acceptance on the basis of the president's electoral mandate. The second example displays a choice between finding legitimacy in the presidential mandate and finding it in the necessity of compromise between the executive and legislative branches.

1. In the last chapter we saw the reluctance of the commissioner of internal revenue to change a decade-old regulation at the request of the Reagan administration when it sought to grant tax benefits to segregated schools. An important reason for this reluctance was a long-term strategy of the IRS. The service has wanted to be accepted as a nonpolitical, quasi-judicial interpreter of the Internal Revenue Code. Accepting the inconsistent role of advocate of presidential priorities would pose considerable strategic dangers for the IRS.

The influence of the commissioner of internal revenue in making tax policy depends largely upon the willingness of Congress, particularly of the Ways and Means and Finance committees, to let stand a wide range of matters of interpretation embodied in IRS rulings and regulations. Much of its influence depends upon similar restraint and deference from the courts, including the Supreme Court. For Treasury to reverse a longstanding ruling at the administration's urging would invite congressional review by (a) admitting uncertainty about the proper interpretation of the law and (b) demonstrating a willingness to change well-established arrangements in the tax area for the president's purposes without the approval of congressional committees that are at least as powerful and active in tax matters as the White House. The same two factors would also reduce judicial deference to the commissioner's position.

Taxpayers have ample financial incentives to appeal questions of interpretation to Congress or the courts if they see a significant prospect of success. If the IRS loses in either forum (an outcome far more likely if it departs from a quasi-judicial role), taxpayers are encouraged to challenge the commissioner's judgment on other matters. The commissioner's long-term stance on the issue of quasi-judicial independence has also won his office a powerful constituency among lawyers and other tax practitioners and thereby erected a wall against pressures by presidents and members of the Congress. It is the central pillar of his strategy for the IRS.

2. A very different choice of the source of legitimacy faced the first chairmen appointed to head the Legal Services Corporation (LSC) at the end of 1981. President Reagan had just lost a major battle in Congress to eliminate federal funding for free legal services for the poor. He could not muster the needed votes. The friends of the Legal Services Corporation on crucial committees in both houses were too numerous; and they also enjoyed the ideological advantage of a broad popular belief that America's pride in law as the basis of order requires the availability of some legal assistance to everyone, including the poor. The fight to maintain funding was vigorously supported by the American Bar Association. The determined opposition of New Right groups supported by David Stockman, director of the Office of Management and Budget, and presidential Counsellor Edwin Meese was roundly defeated.

On most matters the newly appointed chairmen of the Legal Services Corporation—first William Olson and then, after a few months, William Harvey—could proceed only by a majority vote of the board, which was largely appointed by President Reagan. Although critical of the political activities of Legal Services offices across the country, most board members were *not* prepared to abandon the notion of providing some form of legal services to the poor at federal expense. The career staff of the organization in Washington was of course committed to the continuation of federal support, as were the LSC offices throughout the country that did the actual legal work for local eligible clients. These offices maintained close contact with private organizations prepared to monitor carefully everything the new board did and to bring political pressure to bear through willing allies in the Congress and in the press. First organized during the congressional battles of 1981, the supporters of LSC included not only providers and beneficiaries of legal services but also the far more influential and prestigious American Bar Association.

The crucial congressional committees, largely friendly to legal services and suspicious of President Reagan's appointees, could be expected to respond promptly to any board actions threatening to the organization which so many in Congress had just fought so hard to maintain. And they had effective responses to any such threat. Supporters could persuade a majority of each house to restrict the authority of the board to promulgate detailed directives and to order that funding be maintained. The crucial Senate committee could refuse to confirm Reagan's appointees. Having lost on this issue during his powerful legislative "honeymoon," the president might prove unwilling to enter this battle again or unable to bring about any different results.

In this context the leaders of the LSC board, Olson and Harvey, should have seen that one choice confronting them had implications far more sweeping than any other: whether the board would be truly independent of the president and his wishes. The Reagan administration had tried to destroy the Legal Services Corporation in 1981 and failed. Both the New Right (led by Howard Phillips and Gary Curran) and Edwin Meese and David Stockman had made clear that they were totally and unequivocally committed to the elimination of the corporation and that their views were very close to the president's. Now, at last, President Reagan had appointed a board for the corporation, which was charged by statute with being independent of the president and the administration. The central choice facing the board was whether it would visibly adopt the views of President Reagan and his lieutenants or place itself somewhere between that position and the position of the victorious supporters of the corporation in the House and the Senate and in the American Bar Association.

So long as the board appeared to be an agent of the Reagan administration, suspicion and fear would dominate the political environment. Distrusting the motivations of their leaders, the senior staff and the field organizations would resist any efforts to change direction. The private groups and members of Congress who had fought and won crucial battles in 1981 would not allow unconfirmed appointees to destroy what the president had been unable to eliminate; and, without evidence to the contrary, they would suspect that the new board's aim was in fact to destroy the LSC. The more radical members of the legal services community would want to depict Olson and Harvey as tools of the New Right, which would be easier if the chairmen could be goaded into unconsidered statements and actions.

There was, of course, a price to be paid for adopting the more promising course of positioning the board somewhere between the Reagan administration and the liberals on the hill: it might irritate the president. The board members would be criticized by the scornful, impassioned Phillips, Curran, and their New Right allies. The criticism would cut deeply to the extent that Olson and Harvey identified with the same ideological groups and shared working relationships and friendships with them. All this was similar to the problem Mike Pertschuk faced as described in chapter 3.

But the rewards of this choice would also be considerable. Congressional and ABA supporters of the Legal Services Corporation would see the board as a way of helping to preserve the LSC. The senior staff and the field offices might recognize a similar interest in helping the board survive and succeed. Olson and Harvey could then have addressed the problems they considered most serious without being attacked at every move as agents of the president bent on destroying the corporation. They could have enjoyed the help of those who had been with the LSC for some time, while they changed the direction of the corporation in significant ways. And this was the path favored by a majority of the new board.

Olson and Harvey chose instead to act as the president's representatives, with disastrous consequences. They ignored the strategic implications of their decision. Since they had failed to dissociate themselves from continuing efforts to destroy the corporation, any chance of accomplishing their objectives would require prompt, forceful actions. They could not afford to proceed slowly and cautiously. Rather than letting their words and other hints of deep hostility to LSC precede their actions (as they in fact did), they should have acted boldly, immediately picking an LSC president sympathetic to their views, who could be ordered to replace the more moderate senior staff. That much was within the power of the board without political support. To capture a majority of the board for such a housecleaning, it might well have been necessary for the chairmen promptly to invoke the help of the White House despite the legal requirements of independence. Following this strategy, Olson and Harvey would have had to assess carefully exactly what steps could be taken without being overruled by Congress, relying heavily on the availability of a presidential veto.

In all this the chairmen would have had to satisfy themselves that the president wanted, or at least was willing, to continue a battle that he had lost in 1981, although that would involve substantial political costs. (That question is much like a central one for the attorney general in chapter 5.) They would have had to accept the fact that they would never be confirmed by Congress and that every vulnerability to attack would be exploited by their opponents. Every issue would be a fight, and every fight would be a bitter, public one. Perhaps some desired policy results could have been accomplished, but at considerable cost.

Short of adopting such a siege-type strategy, Olson and Harvey could not expect to make progress without separating themselves visibly from the position of the Reagan administration in 1981. They could not replace the president or the senior staff of the LSC without the support of other members of the board. They could not win that support so long as other board members felt they needed help from the LSC staff to orient them to the problems and opportunities the organization faced. More generally, the majority of the board was not prepared to set a course directly contrary to that chosen by the Congress in 1981 and vigorously supported by the American Bar Association. Without the support of their own staff and a majority of the board, and without a determined and energetic White House, Olson and Harvey found all their initiatives subject to immediate and effective congressional attack.

Choosing the role of advocate of the president's views, Olson and Harvey brought about an almost unmitigated series of failures. They lost control of the board (whose decisions controlled the LSC). They embarrassed the president by creating a head-to-head conflict between his board and the Senate—a conflict he could not win. The powers of the board they chaired were supplanted by congressional decisions, leaving the board with little discretion or authority. Neither they nor their colleagues were confirmed. They left under a cloud of near scandal, having furthered few of their objectives except to the extent that the confusion they created weakened the organization they headed.

Who Decides?

The president can, of course, replace an agency head who fails to give whole-hearted support to his views, and this may be the fate of a manager who seeks legitimacy either as a neutral expert, a professional, or an interpreter of the law or as a mediator between the president and the Congress. But the president may not want to remove such an agency head, either because he is glad to shed the responsibility for unpopular choices or because he recognizes the political consequences of challenging the manager's independent power in a particular situation.

The influence of powerful professional constituencies supports the commissioner of internal revenue in his assertion of a quasi-judicial role. Similarly, as Watergate showed, White House interference in the exercise of professional judgment in the Department of Justice as to who should be prosecuted by the federal government raises intense opposition from the press, the public, and the Congress as well as from the bar. With this in mind, in 1979 Attorney General Bell promulgated regulations isolating every prosecutor dealing with an open investigation or prosecution from any direct contact on that matter with either the White House or Congress. Even President Reagan could not afford to deny independence to the inspector general of a major department such as Defense, for that would make him appear indifferent to fraud and waste, with predictable consequences in Congress and at the polls. Public demands for effectiveness support the independence of experts who make judgments on the danger of cigarette smoking or of paraquat, the best way to handle a naval blockade, or how to patrol a dangerous sector of town.

Managers who seek legitimacy by adopting the role of mediator between Congress and the president have less protection against White House demands for loyalty than those whose role is quasi-judicial or expert. Secretary of the Interior Walter Hickel was too independent for President Nixon; HEW Secretary Joe Califano, for President Carter; Secretary of State Alexander Haig, for President Reagan. But President Reagan would have benefited from less partisan leadership at the Legal Services Corporation, for a more independent board might have accomplished *some* of his goals while using up little of his credit.

The president plainly saw such advantages when he selected William Ruckelshaus in 1983 to succeed Anne Gorsuch as head of the Environmental Protection Agency. As we have seen in earlier discussions of this situation, the issue of environmental protection remained immensely popular with the American people, who were deeply skeptical of the president's commitment to that concern. Mismanagement of the EPA had resulted in extremely costly attacks on the administration in the press and broadcast media and on the hill. A new administrator who was perceived to be carrying out the wishes of the White House in a tightly controlled, disciplined, unequivocally loyal manner would have been far less useful to the president's purposes than a figure of obvious independence who would be expected to mediate between sharply competing views with considerable personal discretion. Ruckelshaus was essential to restoring the administration's credibility on environmental issues precisely because of his reputation for independence, for concern for the environment, and for respect for the Congress. He could not be expected to abandon these characteristics; he could afford to demand respect for his independence as a condition of taking the job. His strategy for the EPA, like the White House strategy for ending a painful confrontation, gave central place to the role of creative intermediary between different branches, different policies, and different constituencies.

The Congress, too, can refuse to accept a manager's choice among the three roles (presidential agent; intermediary between president and Congress; and quasi judge, professional, or expert). Members of the Senate committee that had to approve the appointment of Caspar Weinberger as chairman of the Federal Trade Commission in 1970 stressed to him that he had no obligation and should feel no allegiance to the president. The relevant committees of both houses would certainly take that position with regard to many of the responsibilities of inspectors general. That position has some obligations that are direct and unmediated to Congress, or so many in Congress believe. And the Congress may also challenge the effort of an agency manager, generally backed by the president, to put the activities of the agency on a professional, expert, or quasi-judicial basis, that is, out of the realm of partisan politics.

As assistant attorney general in charge of the Criminal Division, I interpreted the policies behind the directives of Attorneys General Bell and

Civiletti—that no one in the White House or the Congress should have any direct contact with those in charge of an ongoing criminal investigation—as carrying over, albeit with reduced force, to White House or congressional efforts to review *past* prosecutorial decisions about political or governmental figures. In the spring of 1980 several angry, curious, or suspicious members of the Senate Judiciary Committee wanted to review a number of decisions not to prosecute particular cases—decisions made over the preceding five years by the Public Integrity Section of the Criminal Division. They sought the testimony of the career prosecutor who headed the section and demanded access to the closed investigative files in those cases.

With the approval of my superiors I refused to comply until we were furnished written guarantees of certain steps designed to assure adequate reason for the request, full committee responsibility for the decision, and protection of the privacy interests of those who had, after all, *not* been charged with any crime. My refusal was intended as a way of saying, "Don't turn decisions about prosecutions into a partisan and political issue; they are professional or quasi-judicial matters." I would not have made closed files or career prosecutors freely available to the White House; I could hardly treat a committee better. Understandably, a majority of the committee saw my actions as a far broader claim that the Criminal Division would not be subject to any effective oversight, would not be accountable. As such, they were a direct challenge to the Senate.

The legislative and executive branches had learned different lessons about legitimacy from Watergate. The executive had decided that investigations and prosecutions of political figures should be independent of presidential concerns, should be based on a professional or quasi-judicial model. The Senate and House had learned to suspect the president and his men; they had little faith in changes in process or structure within the executive branch. For the Congress, Watergate had established the importance of legislative oversight as a check on executive abuse. It had shown the importance of willingness to investigate officials of even one's own party. Oversight was a growing and powerful congressional function. Each committee wanted to show that it was vigorous in exercising its responsibility. And every committee also wanted it to be clear that executive agencies were responsive to Congress and not just to the president.

A manager's strategy for being accorded legitimacy will work only if it is accepted by superiors in the executive branch, including the president, and by the Congress. When the president disagrees, he can overrule the manager's choice of role (at a price), as Reagan did with the reluctant commissioner of internal revenue and acting solicitor general in the case of the segregated schools. When Congress is the stumbling block, the outcome must be compromise. In my encounter with the Senate Judiciary Committee, the committee insisted on its own views of the comparative importance of congressional oversight and professional independence. A dialogue of actions resolved the disagreement.

The committee issued subpoenas and the Senate as a whole endorsed demands for unconditional Criminal Division compliance with the Senate's oversight demands. The department still insisted that certain conditions to protect privacy and prosecutorial independence had to be assured before files were delivered. The committee responded with broader and more unconditional demands. Just as the Judiciary Committee may have believed the department was rejecting any congressional oversight, the department now saw the committee's new demands for far freer access to closed files as an effort to tip the balance between politics and professionalism far to the other side.

The outcome of such a struggle over sources of legitimacy and strategy depends on the nature of the issue and its meaning to the media and special issue constituencies such as, in this case, the bar. If the matters involved look like ones that should be outside politics—left in expert hands or ruled by law or professionals—and there is little reason to suspect a cover-up, Congress is less likely to prevail. If there is some basis for suspecting an effort to hide some form of wrongdoing or other agency vulnerability, and if the matter seems appropriate for politics, the answer is very different, for the costs to the executive branch of resistance are then far higher. In this case, these factors favored the executive. As an extended dispute became burdensome to each side, compromise became attractive to both. An agreement made all the requested files and the testimony of the section's chief attorney available to the Senate committee, but subject to a dozen protective conditions.

The Constraints

Not every question can be presented as appropriate for expert, professional, or quasi-judicial judgment. I know of no better example of this than the decision of Raymond Peck, administrator of the National Highway

Traffic Safety Administration (NHTSA) in the early years of the Reagan administration, about his most politically inflamed subject: whether to require airbags or other passive restraints in every automobile.

The issue had been the subject of forceful and intelligent lobbying by industry and public interest groups for well over a decade. The Congress had vacillated, often in response to unpredicted and perhaps unpredictable public reactions. Administrations differed from each other and often wavered during their own tenure.

During the Carter administration, Secretary of Transportation Brock Adams had promulgated a regulation requiring passive restraints (either airbags or shoulder belts that would automatically connect, unless manually detached, when the door of the car was closed). This decision had overruled a contrary decision by Secretary William Coleman during the Ford administration. The Adams regulation was not to go into effect for several years—until 1981—a delay that had aroused the fury of Ralph Nader.

During the election campaign of 1980 Ronald Reagan sent clear signals of his personal opposition to passive restraint requirements. After his election the same message was conveyed by James Miller, the second in command at the Office of Management and Budget, by Secretary of the Treasury Donald Regan, and even by Secretary of Transportation Drew Lewis. Lewis delayed the effective date of the Adams passive restraint requirement while the matter was reviewed, a decision the automobile manufacturers regarded as significant.

Despite these indications of their views, Secretary Lewis and President Reagan both conveyed to Peck that he was to use his own judgment in making the decision on passive restraints, that is, on relatively costly systems that automatically protected even those drivers who did not take the trouble to connect their seat or shoulder belts. And the views of many in Congress were plainly and sharply opposed to those of the president. Years earlier, Secretary Coleman had estimated that airbags could save nine to twelve thousand lives (and tens of thousands of serious injuries) each year. The cost was high, but the number of lives to be saved was staggering.

Peck's decision would signal the role he wanted his agency to play in this area, what its position was to be with regard to the other great powers—the president and the Congress—in the area of auto safety. There were three possibilities:

1. He could look to politics for the source of legitimacy of his deci-

sions—their staying power and acceptability—choosing a strategy of responsiveness to the president and his policies. If he took this path, there were ample signals as to what decision he should make. The president had campaigned against mandatory passive restraints. The secretary of the treasury and other officials had taken the same position publicly. The decision to delay the effective date of the outstanding regulation requiring passive restraints had sent a clear signal to the automobile manufacturers.

2. A second strategy would depend on a more tenuous sort of political legitimacy. Peck could have placed his agency somewhere between the president and his policies of quite radical deregulation, on the one side, and the supporters of strong regulatory policies for auto safety, on the other. Claiming to be responsive to both sides, the NHTSA would have had maximum independence in its decisionmaking. Legitimacy and acceptance of Peck's decisions would then have been grounded in general recognition of the unavoidable need to compromise between the claims of two politically accountable bodies. He may have known that William Ruckelshaus had successfully followed such a strategy as the first administrator of the Environmental Protection Agency, placing himself between President Nixon and Senator Edmund Muskie.

The president might accept this strategy. It offered him some protection against constituent pressures from the left, though more conservative supporters would complain that he had not held his subordinates on a tighter rein. It depended upon the president being prepared to accept some independence in that part of his administration for its political advantages, disclaiming full responsibility for the actions of a particular agency. If he had adopted this political strategy, Peck could have expected less support and loyalty from the administration but more influence with Congress and thus more bargaining power with the administration than if he defined his role as advocate for administration policy.

3. The third broad alternative was to seek legitimacy as a quasi-judicial, expert decisionmaking body. Such a strategy would involve showing independence from any political influences, presidential or congressional. The strength of Peck's position would depend upon public acceptance of the claimed neutrality, professionalism, and judgelike role. Secretary Lewis and the president had both told Peck they wanted him to adopt this posture with respect to passive restraints. Signals from other powerful figures in the administration were consistent with this message.

The choice among these three positions was the most basic element of

Peck's strategy. It would affect his relationships with the administration, his own staff, Congress, interest groups, and the press. NHTSA was not formally an independent agency, so the choice had to be made, somehow, between Peck and his superiors. It was not a unilateral decision either for the president (unless he was prepared to fire Peck and abandon any pretense of quasi-judicial neutrality in this area) or for Peck (unless he was prepared to ignore his obligation and his dependency as an appointee of the president).

The choice that Peck had to make would importantly influence his relations with those he needed for external support and those he needed to maintain the internal capacity of his organization. Whatever role he chose, it could not simply be announced. Words are unpersuasive. His choice would have to be read from his actions more than from his words. His major decisions would be the cues that others would use to reach their own conclusions as to which of the three postures he had adopted. What his decision would reveal about his broader strategies was something Peck could not ignore as he made a choice on an issue as important as passive restraints.

Peck defined the issue of passive restraints as whether or not to rescind his predecessor's decision. He found that particular decision (the Adams regulation) seriously flawed in light of the current situation. It would allow the automobile manufacturers to comply by furnishing a detachable form of passive restraint—automatically connecting (but manually disconnectable) shoulder belts. Peck reasoned that the manufacturers would prefer this cheaper option, rejecting airbags, and that drivers would then choose to detach the device. As a result of these two steps, nothing would be gained by the Adams requirements. And it would be a costly failure both in consumer dollars and in the credibility of NHTSA.

One did not have to make highly controversial moral judgments about the price that should be paid to save thousands of lives or the proper place of paternalism in government regulation to see that the Adams proposal would no longer work. If the question was whether to maintain or rescind the particular regulation that Secretary Adams had promulgated a few years earlier, the answer could be set forth as almost a technical conclusion. In fact, that was the great advantage of defining the question as he did.

But defining the question in that way was indefensible. Peck never even considered the possibility of ordering that airbags or other nondetachable forms of passive restraint be installed. Nothing in the statute required

NHTSA to allow the manufacturers the option of using detachable restraints.

Peck wanted to reach his decision in a professional way by bringing expert judgment to a technical question. He certainly also thought that his decision was an expression of a strategy for the agency that placed it as an independent, neutral, almost judicial decisionmaker. Whether others would see his decision and his agency in this way would depend upon the adequacy or capacity of technical arguments to resolve such a matter and, extremely importantly, whether the decision was sustained by the courts. A decision labeled arbitrary and capricious by the courts would be hard to defend as a nonpolitical exercise of expert judgment.

All this made the question, To what extent could Peck's decision be made as a technical, expert, nonpolitical matter? a central factor. If the decision could be made in this wholly nonpolitical way (that is, free of widely contested value choices) even if the result were to abandon the requirement of passive restraints, he could expect the decision to survive attacks in a Congress still conservative on regulatory matters. To that extent the matter would be laid to rest. And he would have shifted his organization to a posture of independence and neutrality from a posture of vigorous regulatory advocacy. Perhaps, then, the Congress would be inclined to defer to the agency's views, and the auto safety issues would become less partisan and contentious. On the other hand, if the decision appeared to have important political aspects or if—much worse—it was overruled by the courts as beyond the competence of the agency, it would be far less likely to be permanent, the agency would be viewed as partisan and responsive to the president, and the issue might be far from laid to rest.

Peck defined the question in such a way as to make it turn upon the one aspect of the choice on which expert judgment was central: how private parties, whether automobile manufacturers or users, would respond to a regulation. This was an extremely important aspect of the decision. A showing that a requirement of passive restraints in cars would not work—that they would not be used and therefore would do no good—would be an overwhelming argument against requiring manufacturers to make them standard equipment. What does not work is not politically defensible or socially desirable. Whether people will comply with a regulation and what its effects will be are largely technical questions. Peck's instincts to focus on this issue were dictated by a strategy of making the agency a neutral expert body.

The trouble was that, important as these questions were, they did not encompass enough of the decision before him to make that decision purely or even largely technical. Peck's choice—the one given him by the president and Secretary Lewis—was inescapably political.

The ultimate question of passive restraints is whether everyone in a car should be protected against the effects of accidents or whether, alternatively, those who want protection should have an opportunity, reasonable in cost and availability, to be safe. Requiring airbags might be necessary to accomplish the first purpose; making airbags or lap and shoulder belts inexpensively available to those who want them would be sufficient to accomplish the latter. The choice is one of political philosophy, not of technology.

There were, of course, a variety of alternatives fitting somewhere between these positions and making it somewhat more likely that people would choose to protect themselves without requiring automatic protection. Every car was already required to have seatbelts. Drivers could be required to use them. Secretary Drew's successor, Elizabeth Dole, pressed the states forcefully in this direction. A further step would involve technology that provided protection unless affirmative efforts were taken to disconnect it. It could, in short, be made more or less burdensome to free yourself from the protective devices. But even with these intermediate steps the choice remained for Peck.

He had to resolve the political question whether people should be protected against their own folly or left to suffer the consequences of that folly. No choice is more political in the United States. No technological answer would avoid it. It is because the choice is so political that Congress had entered the area so quickly and with such disconcerting results to Peck and his predecessors. It is because the choice is so political that President Reagan had declared his position on it as part of his electoral campaign. And this is why it had always previously (and since) been vested at the cabinet level in the secretary of transportation.

Peck ignored the political question and, on the basis of technical considerations, simply rescinded the Adams regulation. He did not even consider some alternative regulation not subject to the technical objections that defeated the Adams rule. The court of appeals and the Supreme Court overruled Peck's decision, declaring it "arbitrary and capricious." The Court ruled that Peck was required to address the question whether airbags or other nondetachable restraints should be ordered and that he could not satisfy himself by simply determining that the particular outstanding regulation, the Adams standard, was flawed and should be rescinded. "Given the judgment made in 1977 that air bags are an effective and cost-beneficial life saving technology," the Court held, "the mandatory passive restraint rule may not be abandoned without any consideration whatsoever of an air-bags-only requirement."* Ironically, Peck's unsuccessful effort to deny the political dimensions of the issue left him looking like a mere advocate of administration policy.

There was no technical, professional, or quasi-judicial answer to the decision that was left to Peck. Thus he could not position his agency as one whose decisions should be accepted because of their expert, professional, or quasi-judicial quality. Peck had to choose between the other possible strategies for NHSTA. In doing so, he would find questions of implementation and compliance and matters of technology of great importance to his decision. But ultimately his decision would have to be a political choice made in the light of organizational strategy; and a major ingredient of that strategy would be deciding between the only two remaining, viable sources of legitimacy.

---

*Motor Vehicle Mgfrs. Assoc. of U.S., Inc., et al. vs. State Farm Mutual Auto Ins. Co., et al., 463 U.S. 29, 51 (1983).

7 *Strategic Relations among Organizations Sharing a Common Responsibility*

A Structure of Strategies

The structure of the federal government is generally described with an organizational chart showing the president at the top, under him all the departments and agencies, and within each of these a variety of bureaus and divisions that are themselves composed of sections and offices. This is an accurate picture of the distribution of authority to issue orders and of obligations to obey. But it is misleading insofar as it suggests a process dominated by the setting of policy from above and the carrying out of orders at the lower levels, with the intermediate levels solely responsible for transmission of orders or directions from higher levels and selecting, monitoring, and providing incentives to those at the lower levels. That picture confuses two quite different matters: the distribution of executive authority and the responsibility for choosing the activities and roles of the organization.

Part of the confusion has already been explored. Setting the direction for a government organization involves far more than just discovering the wishes of those higher up in the executive chain of command. Any intelligent choice is made as much in light of the wishes and powers of members of Congress, organized interest groups, wider publics influenced by the media, and the members of the organization itself as in response to superiors. For very good reasons that choice, if made consciously, must be made largely by the leaders of each organizational unit, not by their superiors. The people immediately responsible for the activities of a particular unit know best what problems their programs face, what capacities the organization has, what success it is having, what demands are being made, what power backs them up, and so forth. And they fill in the broad gaps in the overall concerns of their superiors; they have a more complete sense of the needs in the area.

The last point is particularly important. The concerns of the president— his goals and themes and constituencies—bear on only a relatively small part of the total activities of a department. The concerns of the department head, the cabinet secretary, shape only a fraction of the policy at the next division or bureau level. And the same is true on down the line. *Strategy at any level does not fully determine activity at lower levels.* It leaves a great deal of room for discretion, shaped by the strategies of the subordinate organizations.

From the point of view of a higher-level manager, the two crucial requirements for maintaining external support from legislators, interest groups, and wider publics are: (1) to carry out effectively activities of particular concern to these supporters, and (2) to pursue themes external supporters care about, such as economy, honesty, or reduced regulatory demands, in carrying out the activities. The activities and themes win support and build alliances. But, from the point of view of a manager of a lower-level unit, the activities crucial to his superior's external support comprise only a portion of his unit's activities (that is, it does many other important things); and, consistent with broad themes, these activities can still be carried out in a number of importantly different ways.

Of course the higher-level manager also has her own sense of the public's needs in the area (her own objectives) and responsibility to the goals of *her* superiors, which add further definition to the strategy for a particular area. But, as we have seen in the case of a president, these too deal with only a fraction of the open issues as to what the lower-level organization shall do and how it will do it. A higher-level manager, in short, divides matters into those she wants to shape for strategic reasons—either her own objectives and those of her superiors or her and their need for outside support—and the many other matters she wants to leave to others through delegation of responsibility. The decisions of any sizable organization must be made by many people at a number of levels.

But a further confusion fostered by the image of an organizational chart involves an aspect of strategy that has not yet been addressed. It arises from two additional facts. First, activities are not, and cannot be, organized along neatly hierarchical lines with responsibility for each area of activity or work placed cleanly in a single department or bureau. Four or more cabinet-level departments are involved in questions of foreign assistance, and the same is true of law enforcement, welfare benefits, and environmental protection. The president—the only common superior of departments—obviously cannot sort out the innumerable problems of cooperation in the face of potential disagreement about ends or means that flow from this shared responsibility. The need for coordination must often be addressed by horizontal arrangements, not just by orders from above. And second, vigorous organizations sharing responsibility compete with each other for the good things of bureaucratic life.

A satisfactory image of the activity of the federal government would reflect these facts. The picture would show a collection of organizations, each with its own history, tradition, and momentum and each subject to the tugs and pulls of a variety of outside forces. Better yet, imagine hundreds of strategies, more or less well thought out, which must somehow be related to each other and to the politics and plans of the president. Federal activity is made up of interconnecting strategies, with the connections forged and maintained by the managers of units at every level. For each manager the strategy must be a highly complex combination of the needs and responsibilities of: (a) her organization; (b) the larger one of which it is a part; and (c) the other organizations working in the same area.

The Family Traits of Different Organizations Working in the Same Area

The various organizations, often in different departments, sharing a similar responsibility for meeting a social need have their own individual goals. The total governmental involvement in the area of that need is the sum of the activities and themes of a number of federal, state, and local organizations. These organizations are aware that they constitute a group—a rather disorderly family. They recognize that they are part of a loosely structured governmental response to the same general area of needs. Like family members, they develop shared characteristics and an overall group loyalty. Also like family members they develop powerful rivalries and deep divisions that become facts of life taken for granted by all members of the "family." Thus there is a pattern of social understandings and relationships behind the activities of government organizations working in the same field. A background understanding of these realities is a prerequisite of the development of any strategy for a single organization working in the area. The understanding involves both what they share and what divides them.

The manager must, first, come to understand the crucial characteristics *shared* by those, from a variety of organizations, participating in the same enterprise. To what extent are there common goals, shared political vulnerabilities, and similar institutionalized values of the participants? The success of any single organization generally depends upon the success of the entire enterprise and that depends on serving—or changing—the common goals and avoiding the common vulnerabilities. Leadership also follows respect, which can be earned only by serving the group and embodying or reshaping much of its shared values.

Then, just as important, the manager must trace the lines of *division,* suspicion, and rivalry among the organizations and the failures in the common enterprise they cause. Support from sister organizations requires at least taking account of their individual needs and organizational fears. Recognizing gaps in the common enterprise attributable to these is also a crucial clue to finding a needed role.

The manager must find a set of activities that are consistent with the shared goals, values, and vulnerabilities of the organizations in the area (or develop a plan to change these), that are respectful of the major jurisdictional dividing lines (unless or until he has the higher-level support to challenge them), and yet that are obviously needed in the common enterprise. To all this, of course she must add the traditional aspects of strategy necessary to maintain outside and presidential support for whatever set of activities are to be specially associated with her bureau or division.

Consider, as an example of the necessary steps of orientation, the following brief look at the broad field of federal law enforcement. There is nothing special here. The point could as easily be illustrated by the area of foreign assistance or care for the poor, defense or environmental protection, worker and consumer safety, or border control and immigration.

SHARED CHARACTERISTICS

The overriding political fact in law enforcement is that, for obvious reasons, catching, prosecuting, and punishing the perpetrators of crime is, almost always, a very strongly supported and extremely popular government activity. The explanation may be as simple as that the actions made criminal are generally those that a large proportion of the population believes are immoral or, worse, dangerous. Only national defense, which draws on similar fears, commands such universal approval; and law enforcement is far cheaper. Few people distinguish between the targets of federal and local law enforcement. It is in fact almost impossible for most people to determine what matters are getting the attention of different investigative and prosecutorial bodies. So all share to a large extent in the popularity of this form of government activity.

The head of a federal agency working in the area might well note first that widespread popular support as an element common to all participants in the law enforcement effort. But he would also see that there is much less agreement on what types of criminal behavior are worse or which, for some other reason, should receive particular attention. The Ford and Carter administrations had defined the priorities for federal investigation and prosecution as economic crimes (fraud), public corruption, narcotics, and organized crime. These areas were not considered more important than street crime, an area the Reagan administration claimed had somehow been overlooked. Except that it is hardly necessary, a federal theme denouncing violent street crime may be important in terms of what the government *says,* but not in what it *does* through federal investigators and prosecutors. The far larger number of local prosecutors and police can and must address street crime. The Ford and Carter priorities were therefore directed to the areas where state and local law enforcement could not operate as effectively as their federal counterparts for a variety of reasons ranging from conflicts of interest to the availability to the federal government of far more highly trained investigators and sophisticated investigative tools. The federal priority areas were thus the gaps in a joint enterprise that only the federal government could fill.

Beyond this, no one has ever had much success in defining the goals of federal law enforcement. As a practical matter, the object has been to bring as many important cases as possible, where "important" means involving serious wrongdoers or serious wrongs. Even that goal has never been made measurable in useful ways. There are too many variations of what is important; and an effort to specify in Washington what is important runs head on into the powerful claims of the ninety-five U.S. attorneys in ninety-five cities who handle the vast majority of the federal prosecutions and who cherish and protect a tradition of independence based on the mores of the legal profession, their ties to local courts, and the presidential and senatorial roles in their appointment.

Several shared vulnerabilities to longstanding public suspicion demand attention. An organization assigned a goal as powerfully supported as law enforcement (or defense) is always vulnerable to charges of incompetence in carrying out responsibilities that the public and the Congress take so seriously. In most cases no one is likely to know of the specific failures of investigators and prosecutors; still, the demands for competence in the form of vigor and intelligence are very great. Second, granted great powers to deal with matters of great public concern, federal law enforcement is also vulnerable to charges of abuse of those powers. A national tradition of fear of government often focuses on a fear of investigative powers, a fear that is reflected plainly in the Bill of Rights of the Constitution. Finally, there are powerful demands of equality and fairness in subjecting people to such serious harms as flow from investigation and prosecution. Charges of bias or partisanship are thus also an important vulnerability.

The institutionalized values of law enforcement officials reflect these vulnerabilities. Federal prosecutors and investigators want to be the instruments of just punishment for violators of the federal criminal law. They know they are expected to be fair and law-abiding in investigative and prosecutorial activities. They anticipate charges of ruthlessness. They know they cannot show bias on the basis of politics or wealth or relationship to those with power. They fear such accusations most of all, save only charges of personal corruption. They value highly the craft and skill of a talented trial lawyer or investigator and the character traits of toughness, skepticism bordering on cynicism, and aggressiveness that are traditional for law enforcement officials.

Federal prosecutors and investigators are greatly influenced by the courts in which they work. They recognize a special vulnerability to public charges based on judicial determinations that law enforcement officials have disregarded the civil liberties of citizens. More affirmatively, they have a sense that their legitimacy comes from the professional and almost judicial role they themselves play in enforcing the law, with substantial independence from the politics of the president and the Congress, except as these are embodied in statutes or very broad statements of policy.

The various federal agencies have one other matter in common. Although not all investigative agencies are in the Department of Justice, the attorney general has an accepted primacy in the law enforcement world. He is the bureaucratic superior of the most prominent investigative agencies (the FBI and the Drug Enforcement Administration) and all federal prosecutors. To see a case carried through to conviction, those investigative agencies that are not within the Department of Justice must win the support of prosecutors who are under the attorney general. And above all, the attorney general enjoys the status of the highest legal official within the executive branch, with special relationships to courts and the bar and thus with special access to powerful and widespread public support of law and lawful law enforcement as the basis of order.

LINES OF DIVISION

So much for the shared characteristics of the federal agencies working in the area of law enforcement. Their differences and jealousies are equally important. The part of the total set of investigative responsibilities that is entrusted to the inspectors general in major federal departments focuses on fraud against federal programs or procurement and, in particular, the early detection as well as prevention of such fraud. The investigators from the Federal Bureau of Investigation, the Postal Inspectors, the Drug Enforcement Administration, and the Treasury law enforcement offices distinguish their work and skills (investigative or detective work) from that of those in the inspectors general offices (internal control, including auditing, investigation of whatever suspicious circumstances an audit or an allegation reveals, and review of systems) and insist that the inspectors general relinquish control of the later stages of any investigation likely to result in criminal charges. The inspectors general do not agree.

The several investigative agencies involved in high-status criminal work jealously guard from each other their respective jurisdictions, which are defined in terms of particular sections of the federal criminal statutes, although this form of definition works poorly when the same criminal conduct may easily violate several statutes assigned to several different investigative agencies. Overlapping responsibility for narcotics offenses is, for example, a constant source of friction. Even the most prestigious of the investigative agencies, the FBI, must also defend its independence against the current view of prosecutors that *they* should play a very prominent role in directing major investigations. The prosecutors have some power to enforce their view because several crucial investigative tools (electronic surveillance, grand jury subpoenas, immunity orders, and so forth) involve judicial procedures, and here the lawyers play a gatekeeping role.

The federal prosecutors often have less than cordial relationships with their local counterparts, who feel that the federal prosecutors steal the more highly publicized cases, particularly in the field of local public corruption. In New York and many other cities the district attorney and the U.S. attorney have long been in competition with one another for major cases and public acclaim. There are also important divisions within the ranks of the federal prosecutors. U.S. attorneys will vie for responsibility for any major investigation or prosecution. Subsequent careers in private life turn on the outcome. They will vigorously protect their turf, with the aid of local judges, against the invasion of a federal prosecutor from Washington. For years, until the late 1970s, there had been bitter conflict between the Washington-headed Organized Crime Strike Forces, scattered in major cities around the country, and the U.S. attorneys in those cities. U.S. attorneys simply did not like the presence in their districts of investigators and prosecutors pursuing highly popular cases for which the U.S. attorney got no credit.

It is by no means clear that anyone less than the attorney general or deputy attorney general, neither of whom has a sizable personal staff, has much authority to press uniform procedures or priorities on the ninety-five U.S. attorneys, generally appointed because of the support of a senator from the state. The most powerful of these—for example, the U.S. attorney for the Southern District of New York—occupy offices whose independence is protected by history and powerful alumni, as well as by a reputation for professional excellence and sheer talent that few other federal offices can claim.

The Implications for a Single Organization of Shared Responsibility

THE IMPORTANCE OF WHO DOES WHAT

In earlier chapters I have emphasized the questions: what shall the manager of an organization do and say about its goals, how might that change over time, in what manner and with what vulnerabilities are the activities carried out, and by what authority or claim of legitimacy does the manager bolster the acceptability of his or her decision? What must be added now to these matters of what and how is the question, who? For who does what bears importantly on a number of the other aspects of strategy previously considered. Consider four crucial aspects: what results are accomplished, what external support is enjoyed, with what enthusiasm and capacity does the organization undertake its mission, and what problems of political vulnerability and benefits of legitimacy accompany the effort?

The first point is entirely obvious. There may be substantial benefits of cooperation with other agencies in terms of results that can be achieved. Together the Departments of State and Justice can handle immigration better than either could alone. The uncoordinated distribution of cash and food benefits to the poor by different departments seemed an obvious inefficiency to President Nixon in 1970. The Departments of State, Treasury, and Commerce must coordinate their efforts to shape our economic relations with Mexico. More rarely, there are grave risks of cooperation. The chance of a breach of secrecy increases with the number of parties involved. For this reason federal law enforcement agencies are extremely reluctant to cooperate with local agencies in some forms of investigation, such as charges of public corruption. The intelligence agencies are often reluctant, for similar reasons, to cooperate with law enforcement agencies.

The question, Who will carry out this responsibility? also bears importantly on that aspect of strategy that seeks to guarantee external support for the organization. Taking on a new activity that is highly valued by elected officials (because it seeks to deal with a subject of significant concern to them or one where there is much popular interest and demand for action) tends to garner additional resources and, when the public cares, valuable constituent support. Maintaining that external support depends, of course, upon carrying out the new responsibilities well. The FBI has, for example, enjoyed important support from banking institutions and from legislators responsive to them because of the importance they attach to problems of bank robbery and embezzlement and because of the success of the FBI, over a sustained period, in dealing with these matters. Periodic efforts by attorneys general to turn that responsibility over to local authorities on the ground that it does not require the special talents of the FBI are regularly resisted because of the loss in external support that would result.

Simply expanding an agency's responsibilities is not a sensible way of gaining additional external support. The new responsibilities have to be highly valued; and the organization must be capable of carrying them out effectively. Since external support is crucial and scarce, agencies often compete for work considered important by those who can furnish that support. It is a simple fact of life that the president, other common superiors, and the Congress must and will avail themselves of the opportunity to give various agencies differing amounts of authority, jurisdiction, appropriations, and deference depending upon the importance they attach to that part of the shared jurisdiction assigned to each agency and according to their evaluation of the skill with which salient responsibilities are carried out.

Third, the capacity of the manager to manage and to command the loyalty of those in her organization depends upon both their view of her success in this competition among agencies and, closely related, their sense that what they are doing is highly valued by the public, the press, the president, and the Congress. These matters will affect recruits and transfers as well as the enthusiasm of those who are now in the agency. Still, it is far too simple to assume that the internal capacity and inclinations of the organization are always furthered by growth and expanding responsibilities. Obviously, at a minimum, its resources must expand to meet new responsibilities or the organization is likely to pay the price, in terms of morale, of a staff spread too thin and of failures in other areas of its activities.

As I argued in the case of the Department of Justice, part of the strength of an organization is also its sense of a coherent identity, which tends both to socialize and unify its members and to provide a particular claim to deference in handling some aspects of responsibility shared by several organizations. Taking on new responsibilities can threaten that organizational identity. The work of drug enforcement agents is quite different from the work of most FBI agents; for many years that difference gave directors of the FBI some pause when suggestions were made that the FBI begin to handle drug cases, as it now has. Prosecutors have different attitudes and are expected to have different relationships with their litigating opponents from those appropriate for lawyers handling civil matters. Absorbing a substantial civil litigating jurisdiction would be a questionable undertaking for the Criminal Division of the Department of Justice.

Finally the prospect of answering, who is responsible for this area? by describing a scheme of cooperation presents the opportunity to overcome the political vulnerabilities that are special to a single organization and to bolster claims of legitimacy. Like almost every police agency, the Federal Bureau of Investigation is particularly vulnerable to charges of disregarding the civil liberties of citizens. Perhaps because of the close personal and political relationship between most presidents and their attorneys general, the Department of Justice is, generally unfairly, vulnerable to charges of favoring the wealthy or the well-connected. Joint involvement in an activity can protect each organization against the appearance of failing to carry out its responsibilities in an acceptable way. The approval of lawyers in the department makes it harder to charge the FBI with disregard of civil liberties; the involvement of professional, career agents makes less credible charges of political bias in Justice. Working together the two organizations have a stronger claim to the independent authority of professionalism in law enforcement. In sharp disagreement, such claims to the legitimacy of professional neutrality disappear.

Having in mind the major implications of alternative answers to, Whose responsibility is this? each agency among a set that share power and responsibility can seek any of three distinct relationships with its sister organizations. First, it can seek the benefits of cooperation in results, external support, and legitimacy by allying itself with one or more others in an ongoing field of activity or, more cautiously, in a single endeavor where each has something to gain by an implicit trade. Second, it can decide that the prospects of cooperation with certain agencies are not good, that jurisdictions should be sharply defined, boundaries respected, and distance kept. Third, an agency may recognize with respect to another organization that their roles are too similar and their activities too redundant for the organizations to be anything other than rivals, with the future of each dependent upon its competitive display of relative capacity and the loyalties it elicits from common superiors, the president, or the Congress. This has, for example, often been the understanding between the National Security Council's staff and the Department of State. More often than not, it is also true of the Department of State and the Department of Defense in the area of arms control.

A CONCRETE EXAMPLE

Consider a dramatic example of the importance of the "who" dimension of strategy in the field of law enforcement. Let me begin with the "what" and the "how" dimensions of the quite remarkable ABSCAM investigation. An investigation of forged securities and other crimes of financial fraud and art swindles was initiated in Brooklyn by the local office of the FBI, relying extensively on an extremely clever confidence man named Melvin Weinberg, who had become an informant after being convicted in a federal court in Pennsylvania. Wondering whether organized crime figures might be involved in the recently legalized gambling in Atlantic City, the FBI encouraged its informant, Weinberg, to ask how he might go about getting a license for a casino on behalf of his purported principals, wealthy Arab sheiks. He was told the mayor of Camden, New Jersey, could handle the matter for a fee. So the FBI operatives, who by now were working closely with prosecutors from the Organized Crime Strike Force located in Brooklyn, met with Mayor Angelo Errichetti.

The mayor led them not only to a casino commissioner but also to a variety of other politicians, beginning with Senator Harrison Williams of New Jersey, who was prepared to exchange his help in selling titanium to the Department of Defense for a mammoth loan to a titanium corporation with which he was connected. With the help of Weinberg, Errichetti, and a few other unknowing middlemen, the investigation soon centered on high-level legislative corruption. A half-dozen congressmen from New York, New Jersey, Pennsylvania, South Carolina, and Florida were prepared to sell their influence on immigration matters for cash. Finally the investigation moved to Philadelphia, where several city councilmen could be bribed to help with city permits.

When managers in the FBI and the Department of Justice allowed the ABSCAM investigation to focus on political corruption and particularly on the United States Congress, they were putting a final seal on a major change in direction for law enforcement. Only five years earlier, in the aftermath of Watergate, President Ford had added public corruption to the high priorities of law enforcement officials. Attention to white-collar crime was greatly expanded at the same time. At the beginning, as a result of these steps, federal attention was focused on corrupt local officials and con men, like the informant Weinberg himself.

The major strategic issue with regard to corrupt local officials was whether this area should be left to local district attorneys, for it hardly ever involved investigation in more than one state or sophisticated investigative resources unavailable to local governments. Still there was an adequate rationale for major federal intervention in this area: the possible conflicts of interest when locally elected district attorneys are asked to prosecute other local political figures. At least so it seemed to the federal prosecutors and investigators; their local counterparts have always been far less enthusiastic, since every successful federal prosecution reduces somewhat their prestige and support in the local community and every successful local prosecution by a district attorney expands that support. In 1986, typically, U.S. Attorney Rudolph W. Giuliani and District Attorney Robert Morgenthau were wrestling for control of major investigations of corruption in New York City government.

The ABSCAM investigation took a final major step in defining the strategy that President Ford had begun. Its targets, when it turned to political figures, were people of national status and power. Law enforcement officials take pride in a willingness to go after powerful officials, since it forcefully confirms a highly valued aspect of their self-image and refutes hated charges of bias, favoritism, or corruptibility. But the investigation would look very different to honorable legislators on the hill. Many members of both houses of Congress would suspect partisan motives, fear hostile executive intentions, and resent the unprecedented length and scale of the investigation. And the fear, suspicion, and resentment would have an opportunity to play out against a vulnerability arising from the "how" aspect of the activity. The prominent role played by the con man, Melvin Weinberg, and the willingness to make cash offers to legislators as to whom the primary basis of suspicion was the word of crooked friends or acquaintances that they would be receptive—these would raise civil liberties issues of a sort wise law enforcement officials are very sensitive to.

Altogether, the shift to federal legislative figures in the ABSCAM investigation inevitably declared a shift in strategy for the law enforcement agencies involved. Widespread public approval would have to guarantee the needed external support as the agencies for a time charted a course far more independent of the Congress than had been true in the past. A parallel investigation of judicial corruption in the courts of Cook County ("Greylord") carried many of these same themes. And it too involved serious questions of "how," since a judge's chambers were to be "bugged" and undercover operations were to be used in connection with litigation. It is important to see how central the "who" questions are in the playing out of this dramatic, though brief, new strategy. Consider the historic divisions scarcely below the surface of this investigation.

Until a very few years before the ABSCAM investigation there had been extremely serious conflicts between the Organized Crime Section of the Criminal Division, which reported to the assistant attorney general in Washington, and the U.S. attorneys in the fifteen or so cities where the section's Strike Forces (its field offices) were located. This is hardly surprising. The Strike Forces brought highly regarded cases that were appreciated by the public and the Congress. In doing so they developed particularly close relations with the investigative agencies on which the U.S. attorneys also had to rely. Some peace had been accomplished by an agreement to share credit with the U.S. attorneys and to preserve rather strict jurisdictional lines. Thus ABSCAM, a public corruption investigation of the sort generally assigned to U.S. attorneys, carried from its inception the potential of conflict between the Organized Crime Section's Strike Force in Brooklyn, which had assumed responsibility for monitoring, assisting, and reviewing the undercover investigation, and the affected U.S. attorneys.

When attorneys based in Brooklyn and investigators from New York began handling cases in New Jersey, a second major question necessarily arose. Successful prosecution of prominent New Jersey politicians by any federal prosecutor other than the New Jersey U.S. attorney would raise questions about his competence or his dedication to his job. The questions might be unfair—and they were—but they would still be damaging. The U.S. attorney would fight such an invasion of his jurisdiction. Third, given the division between federal and local jurisdictions, local prosecutors in Philadelphia would be likely to resent a federal focus on local politicians engaged in quite local forms of corruption. And, last, in any major investigation such as this two unresolved sets of questions of leadership return: Is the investigation to be run by the investigators (the FBI) or by the prosecutors (the Organized Crime Strike Force attorneys)? and is it to be run from the field or from headquarters?

Look for a minute at the potentials for alliances and rivalries to reap or waste the benefits of cooperation and to deal with or exacerbate the fear of overreaching. These became central questions of organizational strategy for the participants. If someone is going to declare that it is perfectly all right for law enforcement officials to go rather energetically after members of the Congress too ready to accept bribes and to do this using undercover techniques required for corruption investigations but on a previously unexplored scale, it had best not be the often feared Federal Bureau of Investigation unless it has the clear and strong support of the lawyers in the Department of Justice. Very quickly the agents in Brooklyn developed a very close working relationship with Tom Puccio, the chief of the Organized Crime Strike Force there, and William Webster, director of the FBI, shared responsibility with me as head of the Criminal Division in the

Department of Justice. That investigator-attorney cooperation was plainly essential politically as well as technically.

Consider a less obvious issue in integrating organizational strategies. Corruption investigations were generally the work of the U.S. attorneys, not of the Organized Crime Strike Force. If the Brooklyn Strike Force was going to take charge of this investigation, and particularly, as events unfolded, if the investigation were to cross well-established boundary lines of respect for other jurisdictions, invading the territory of the U.S. attorney in New Jersey, then some effort had to be made to prevent a reoccurrence of the massive divisions and conflicts of the recent past, which pitted federal prosecutors from the Organized Crime Section against those assigned to the U.S. attorney. A prompt alliance between the U.S. attorney in Brooklyn and the Strike Force in that district could and did prevent any division along historical lines. Conflicts between the Brooklyn Strike Force and the New Jersey U.S. attorney remained limited to matters of geographic jurisdiction, not reopening older and far wider divisions between U.S. attorneys and Strike Forces.

The last major "who" question involved relations among geographically limited agencies sharing responsibility: particularly Brooklyn and New Jersey. This division could have been resolved by: a cooperative operation involving prosecutors and investigators from both jurisdictions, simply respecting traditional geographic boundaries, or all-out rivalry for the crucial support of common superiors. It ended in a bitter rivalry, fought out first within the Department of Justice and then in judicial and legislative arenas. Behind the disagreement were important substantive differences about what should be done as well as differences about who should do it. The former differences are generally resolved by simply deciding who is in charge. That is a crucial function of decisions on jurisdiction. Inflamed rather than mollified by the allocation of responsibility for the investigation, the New Jersey prosecutors brought their most severe criticisms about how the investigation was carried out—the dangers they thought it posed to civil liberties—very forcefully to the attention of both courts and Congress in the heated aftermath of ABSCAM.

What I am suggesting is that, for each of the parties that could claim some responsibility for the ABSCAM investigation (the Brooklyn Strike Force, the U.S. attorney in Brooklyn, the FBI agents in Brooklyn, the U.S. attorney in New Jersey, the FBI agents in New Jersey, the Criminal Division in Washington, the FBI Headquarters in Washington, the U.S. attorney in Philadelphia, and the Philadelphia district attorney), strategic choices had to be made about which of the others should be treated as allies or trading partners, or kept at a distance with a scrupulous respect for boundaries, or recognized as rivals and dealt with accordingly. These decisions involve the costs and benefits of cooperation in work. Help is often welcome but sometimes too many cooks can spoil the broth. They also involve the scarcity of external support and the rewards of carrying out a valued responsibility well and effectively.

Each organization had to assess the effect of the demands for time and resources that come with a new responsibility and the rewards of success or failure. Each had to decide whether new activities would be likely to compromise the clarity and integrity of the organization's identity and mission. (The chief of the Organized Crime Section in Washington, for example, worried that the scale of this investigation of public corruption and the absence of organized crime involvement might deflect his unit from its highly valued central purpose.) These organizational decisions involved seeking complementarities in dealing with the areas in which different organizations were vulnerable and trying to find ways to build the legitimacy of central decisions by combining the claims of acceptability of the various participants. (For example, while the investigation was proceeding, the Criminal Division and FBI Headquarters were together producing new administrative guidelines for the proper handling of all major undercover investigations.)

What each organization involved in ABSCAM had to decide was the set of questions that together define, for any organization working in the area of shared responsibilities, that part of its strategy which involves developing a fit with the strategies of the others.

PART II
The Management
of
Politics

8 A Closer Look at the Hill

The Importance of Understanding the Legislative Process

No part of the political environment facing the manager of a government agency is more important or more complex than the legislature. Each one of the variety of ways that his organization and its programs can be affected by statutes or committee actions is a reason why the federal manager must come to understand something about the workings of Congress.

A committee can hold oversight hearings, within its jurisdiction, exposing the failures or improprieties of a government agency and its managers. The EPA and Anne Gorsuch paid this price. It can recommend and the Congress may adopt legislation reducing the powers of an agency. The National Highway Traffic Safety Administration was forbidden by statute to require automobile manufacturers to produce cars that would not run unless their seat belts were in use. The appropriations committees can recommend limitations on the use of money to accomplish particular substantive purposes. Michael Pertschuk at the Federal Trade Commission was eventually forbidden to spend money on rule making in the area of children's television; years before the Reagan attacks, the Internal Revenue Service had been forbidden to spend money promulgating new rules denying tax benefits to segregated schools.

The Congress may pass laws specifying how programs or agencies will be organized or managed. The creation of inspectors general who were to report directly to the Congress and were placed in a number of federal agencies provides an example. The Congress can require, authorize, or prohibit any particular activity or create a new agency to take over an agency's responsibilities. It can, by failing to authorize or appropriate, bring an agency or a program to a close.

Of course it is not quite accurate to say that the Congress can do these things, for the president must approve whatever is done by law (rather than mere inaction). More specifically, the Congress can at any time send the president a bill intended to redirect the activities of an agency or the focus of a program. For this reason alone, the manager of a government agency needs a better understanding than I have so far provided of how legislation works. Somehow the manager must come to have a sense of the Congress that is adequate to protect her from greatly exaggerating or failing to see the influence that a committee or a member can bring to bear on her organization. Of course, there is another side to the relationship as well. It is to the Congress that the manager must look for increased authority, desired legislation, and more funding. With the approval of the Office of Management and Budget, the manager can go to Congress for help, but a prerequisite is understanding the process.

THE METHOD AND MODEL

All this justifies—even requires—an effort to develop a a handy model, a thumbnail sketch, of the legislative process. The simplest way is to invite the manager to place herself, for the next two chapters at least, in the position of a legislator. Of the many contexts that are relevant to the relationship between the manager of a government agency and the Congress, I will use only one in these chapters: floor battles over the authorization and appropriation of funds for an agency. In this chapter the example is domestic, the Legal Services Corporation; in the next, it is that plus a matter of defense policy.

The advantage of using authorizations and appropriations to describe legislative tactics is that this part of the annual congressional cycle is obviously of fundamental importance to government managers. The scarce time in committee and on the floor of each house is already committed to considering the agency's activities at that time; so efforts to redirect the course of the agency's management are most likely then. Rarely will the direction take the form of legislation, rather than oversight or expressive adjustments in funding; but if it does, the president's power to veto an unwanted direction is compromised because he may need the authority and funding provided in the same bills just to keep the agency running.

There are, however, grave risks in the type of thumbnail sketch that follows. For one, the Congress of the United States is a vastly complicated institution. To understand its history, processes, incentives. strengths, and failings is a lifetime work. And very talented people have devoted lifetimes to that task. For another, a thumbnail sketch will, almost inevitably, distort the crucial feelings of the person inside the legislative role: the responsibility to constituencies, the responsibility to the nation, the pride in one's house of Congress, the sense of the special importance of the legislative branch to a popular democracy, the role of personal friendships and loyalties to colleagues, and even the atmosphere of hectic, demanding responsibility where one's own time is the scarcest resource and trust in personal staff is essential. All of this inevitably gets lost in a short, cold model designed for those who are not really part of the legislative process or who are part of it only occasionally.

There are problems no less serious with the use of a single type of occasion and, in particular, floor battles over authorizations and appropriations as the vehicle for explaining the business of legislation. For one thing, discussing these parts of the process without including the related budget process is problematic. Most obvious, the vast majority of the occasions on which a government manager deals with the Congress do not involve spirited floor fights. Therefore more practical advice might focus on giving testimony at a hearing or meeting with a representative or senator in his office to discuss a piece of proposed legislation. What justifies my attention to floor battles is that understanding the conditions of winning a majority of both houses and having the president sign a bill is essential to understanding both the power of individuals in other, less combative contexts and the prospects of particular types of policies—matters that I will explore more fully in chapters 10 and 11.

There is even distortion in the radically simplifying device of inviting the government manager to think of herself, for the next two chapters, as in the legislature. Even in the event of a major battle, what the representatives of the executive branch can and should do differs substantially from the far fuller range of tactics available to a legislator. But all this is the price of brevity. With those warnings, let me proceed.

THE SIX STEPS OF THE MODEL

In the chapters that follow I shall be developing a simplified model for a government manager trying to understand the Congress. It has six steps.

Within a single house (the Senate or the House of Representatives) the starting place is with the set of considerations that move legislators and influence voting decisions. The next step is to note that of all the activities engaged in by sponsors and opponents of a particular piece of legislation—meeting and talking to colleagues, finding allies in the house, using the support of interest groups on the outside, taking advantage of the rules, winning the support of crucial committees, choosing the occasion for crucial votes, designing or negotiating about the form of the proposal, and so forth—some are more important than others because they affect more members in terms of more of the concerns that move legislators.

The third step of the argument is that both sides in the legislative contest will give special attention to the more powerful levers, but different parties on different sides of an issue enjoy different advantages in this regard. Supporters of a proposal may have the benefit of a favorable committee in the House. Their side of the issue may more readily draw the sympathies of a particular, well-organized interest group. Opponents may have the advantage in timing that flows from a recent scandal somehow related to the proposal and the advantage in procedure or process of a friendly Senate committee.

This suggests a quite useful way to define tactics, which is illustrated in chapter 9. Legislative tactics involve identifying the advantages that supporters and opponents of a measure have in reaching and influencing members who will vote on the floor and then devising steps to neutralize your opponents' advantages and to exploit your own. The advantages depend on the precise contours of the proposal and on its timing. They also depend upon who occupies strategic positions on the various paths that the proposal might follow in the established process for decision.

The fourth and fifth steps flow naturally from this definition of tactics. If tactics are the exploration of advantages, then the creation and maintenance of such advantages over time is true political farsightedness. It is a large part of the management of politics. Thus, it is important to examine the nature of the advantages that various individuals enjoy in winning their way in legislative contests and to explore that part of legislative behavior and long-term strategy for an individual that involves building personal advantages or resources of influence. That is the focus of chapter 10.

Not just individuals but also certain policies (such as social security and medicare) enjoy long-term advantages either because those favorable to them occupy positions of power or because they are supported by long-lasting attitudes and beliefs of interest groups or broader concerned publics. Understanding the nature of these advantages, the task of chapter 11, opens up the possibility of taking actions designed to increase the long-run advantages of one set of policies and to decrease those of another. For example, the tax advantage of a depletion allowance for oil was secure as long as the Speaker of the House and the chairman of the House Ways and Means Committee were committed allies of oil interests, the chairman exercised great control over the other members of the committee, and the House Rules Committee (influenced by the Speaker) prevented challenges to the recommendations of Ways and Means on the floor.

A concerted effort by liberal Democrats in the House to change the last two conditions, through exercise of the powers of the Democratic majority meeting in caucus, altered radically the advantages the depletion allowance enjoyed as an issue in the House of Representatives and thus in the Congress. Thereafter the allowance was substantially eliminated. What was necessary was farsighted management of politics, for no short-term effort addressed only to the policy and not to the conditions that made it almost invulnerable could carry the day.

The last, sixth step in the model is different from the others. Understanding the rules of the game that are the skeleton on which legislative muscle hangs is a way of seeing the whole, but it is also a crucial, separate tactic. Crucial rules and precedents shape the entire process from the earliest decisions about what committee shall be responsible for a proposal to the final stages when a bill faces conference and then presidential approval or veto. They establish and specify the very capacity to change the rules themselves. No part of legislative tactics is more important than understanding how rules constrain choices—how they sometimes provide the power to obstruct and, on other occasions, make it possible to surmount obstructions. So, to understand the broadest framework for legislative choice and the anatomy that explains the other steps in the thumbnail sketch as well as to reveal the special strategic importance of sheer mastery of the rules, I will begin there.

The Rules of the Game of Authorization and Appropriation

The compact model—the thumbnail sketch—whose steps I have just described centers in a single house. Even in that context it would be wise to begin with serious attention to the rules that broadly direct legislative activity. Because the rules of the House and the rules of the Senate are extremely complicated, anyone anxious to affect or understand legislative battles must have command of them. The masters of the rules have always been powerful and highly respected figures in each house. And some of the most important rules draw the boundaries between authorizations and appropriations.

Beyond this, some centrally important rules are concerned with the relationship among the two houses and the president. Legislation—whether granting or withdrawing powers, changing organizational structure or management, or providing, limiting the use of, or withholding money—requires the action of both houses and the signature of the president. Any of these three parties can, of course, decline to act; and a failure to authorize an agency's continuing existence or to appropriate money will bring the agency and its programs to an abrupt close. Even in the context of a threat to refuse to take the steps necessary to continue operations, however, the point is the same. A legislator must take account of the rules relevant when the other house or the president may be reluctant to act.

THE RULES

Thus, our starting point is to review the surprisingly intricate rules of the game of authorization and appropriation. Consider the example of President Reagan's effort to eliminate the Legal Services Corporation during his initial ''honeymoon'' period in 1981. A government expenditure for legal services programs, like most others, generally requires both: (1) an authorizing statute, which would be considered first by the committees responsible for legislating or making policy in the area (in the case of legal services, the Judiciary Committee in the House and the Labor and Human Resources Committee in the Senate) and then (2) an appropriating statute, which is recommended by the committees responsible for spending money (the appropriations committees). The authorizing statute may approve the program for several years; an appropriation will usually be for only a single year. The authorization generally sets a ceiling on the amount that can be spent; the appropriation specifies the precise amount within that limit.

Both House and Senate must pass a bill in identical form before it can be presented to the president for signature. Appropriations always begin in the House; authorizations can begin in either body. When both houses have acted and, very often, produced somewhat different bills, the differences are eliminated by the following process. The chair and senior members of the committee—which committee depends on whether it is an authorization or an appropriation as well as the subject matter of the legislation—in each house are generally appointed by the leadership to represent that house at a conference with the other house. The conferees must compromise and give up something that their house had initially passed in order to reach agreement. The proposals of the conferees, once they have produced a single bill, are then voted on separately in each house. A failure to give great deference in each house to the recommendations of the Conference Committee would obviously create a nightmare of a bargaining situation. So the Conference Committee recommendations are generally accepted, though there are notable exceptions. The leaders of each house's team of conferees are expected to fight for the view of their house and are measured by their success.

Within each house authorization bills and appropriations bills are kept in separate categories. Rules and understandings maintain a division of labor between authorizing/legislating committees, which set policy by legislating, and the appropriations committees, which set funding levels. The appropriations committees will not generally provide money for programs that have not previously been authorized by a legislative committee (such as the Judiciary Committee) and will not otherwise legislate in an appropriations bill (as by ordering a department to do something). To enforce this, a rule of the House of Representatives (which takes this division of responsibility more seriously) provides that any legislation in appropriations bills is out of order and thus can be challenged by any single member by a point of order. If that challenge is sustained by the presiding officer, the matter is withdrawn from consideration without any further vote.

An appropriations committee may, without "legislating," deny an agency authority to spend money for a particular purpose (such as to promulgate new regulations about children's television or the taxation of segregated private schools or to assist Contras in Central America). But it cannot change existing laws or impose additional or affirmative duties on officials in the executive branch. Giving initial consideration to such directives or to the desirability of a program is solely within the jealously guarded jurisdiction of the legislative committees.

Of course neither house will allow itself to be painted into a corner by any such rule. There are ways to get around it when a majority of the house wants to, despite the recognized importance of maintaining the power and responsibility of the legislating committees. For example, the House of

Representatives can, on the recommendation of its Rules Committee, simply preclude the raising of any point of order as part of a regulation of the terms and conditions of floor debate. In this way, appropriations bills are passed when the authorization process has become stalemated in conference by a disagreement between the House and Senate legislating committees and a majority agrees that the program must be allowed to continue.

Sometimes neither an authorization bill nor an appropriation bill has been passed by the time a new fiscal year begins on October 1 and, with the new year, the authority of an agency to spend money expires. A few years ago the major reason for this occurrence would be simply busyness and a failure to meet that deadline. To avoid the agency having to shut down, which would be required without statutory authorization of funding, both houses would then pass a "continuing resolution" and send it to the president for signature. Often functioning as both an authorization and an appropriation, it would generally cover a short period of time and specify approved spending levels in a few lines referring to the prior year or the level approved by the House or the Senate.

More recently, both the burdens and delays of the new budget process and prolonged debate about controversial amendments involving busing, school prayer, and abortion have blocked the passage of important appropriations bills. Even a few Senators can filibuster an appropriations bill, holding it hostage to passage of such amendments, because of the traditional reluctance of the Senate to cut off debate and the rules making this somewhat difficult. The use of a continuing resolution has become the familiar device for dealing with this problem too. At the same time the continuing resolution has become much more elaborate in its specification of levels of funding and restrictions on how money can and should be spent in each of a number of areas that, for one reason or another, has no appropriation at the end of a fiscal year. Some agencies, like the Legal Services Corporation, have operated for years under a continuing resolution without either an authorization bill or a separate appropriations bill. The continuing resolution is fashioned by the appropriations committees and their subcommittees, more specifically by their chairs.

An authorization for the Legal Services Corporation or for any other program is likely to be relatively narrow, dealing with only that subject. An appropriations bill may fund a number of agencies and a number of programs. A single continuing resolution, the broadest, may fund a very large part of the entire federal government. Obviously the stakes are much higher, the costs much greater, if someone tries to block a continuing resolution than if the target is an authorization or an ordinary appropriations bill. This prevents the use of the filibuster on a continuing resolution. More important, the president may find it extremely difficult to veto a continuing resolution. Much of the federal government would have to shut down in many cases, since the president cannot veto a part of a bill and the power that President Nixon had asserted to fail to spend (to impound) funds was severely restricted by the Budget Act of 1974.

TACTICAL IMPLICATIONS

These are the most important rules of the game for creating or maintaining or for eliminating or weakening a government program or agency in the regularized process of review involving authorizations and appropriations. Several matters are of obvious strategic important to the legislator concerned to help or harm a program and agency. First, recognizing that the power of committees to influence the vote in the house to which they report is very great, a legislator must consider whether he should set forth his proposal through the authorization process with its committees or through the appropriation process.

In 1981 when there was a powerful demand for unusual budget cuts, those controlling the budget process used the authorization stage to accomplish massive cuts—by setting very low and therefore binding ceilings on expenditures—over the vigorous objection of the appropriations committees with primary responsibility for setting spending levels. On other occasions, as we have seen, when legislative restrictions on an agency have been stalemated by the loyalty of the authorizing/legislating committee in one or both houses, ways have been found to impose the restrictions as part of the appropriations process. Perhaps most important, any stalemate that threatens authorization of an agency's continued existence is likely to be overcome in the context of appropriations.

Second, the powers of the conferees charged with reconciling the differing positions of the House and Senate are formidable in two ways. The conference is the context in which the members of one house, or particular members of that house, can most readily force the other house to adopt a particular proposal. For example, in the late 1970s Senator Pete Domenici, then a minority member of the Senate Committee on Public Works, wanted to impose user charges on barge traffic to help finance the cost of work on inland waterways by the Army Corps of Engineers. His counterparts in the House were likely to oppose such new fees, especially after hearing from the barge interests. Domenici's best prospect for influencing the House of Representatives, of which he was not a member, was as a Senate conferee. In that context, with the support of his Senate colleagues, he could demand agreement to his proposal as part of the process of reconciliation of differing bills that included funding for various public works particularly popular in the House.

The other power of conferees is the converse of the power to demand; it is the power to recede or give in. In 1973 when the very junior congressman Les Aspin persuaded the House to vote a lower ceiling on certain defense expenditures against the recommendation of the House Armed Services Committee, senior committee members were still able to have their way by simply dropping Aspin's undesired amendment as one of the concessions they made to the Senate conferees, for the Senate bill was more to their liking on this point. A great power of senior committee members is to decide which of their house's proposals will be defended less vigorously than others in conference.

Finally, a presidential veto or a threat of veto can play any of several crucial roles. Only some powers, authority, and funding disappear routinely unless a new statute is passed. Others can be eliminated only by a statute, and if the president wants to retain power or authority in the latter category, he need only veto the legislation and find one-third of the members of either house to sustain his veto. A threat of veto can, if it is credible, eliminate a major piece of legislation or a part of that legislation. Despite widespread concern after President Reagan's reelection in 1984 about huge budget deficits, concern shared by crucial congressional leaders, none of the effort required for a tax increase was made in either house, for the politically costly process would be futile in light of the president's promised veto.

Less obviously, a credible threat of a veto can help add a measure to a piece of legislation or provide a bargaining chip to force enactment of a separate measure. In the case of the waterways bill that Senator Domenici pressed, his hopes of enacting a user fee depended upon the strong desires of a majority of each house to pass various public works authorizations to which Senator Domenici had linked his proposal. A simple amendment in either house could have separated the popular authorization of public works from the highly controversial charging of user fees. But Senator

Domenici persuaded President Carter to threaten to veto any bill that authorized the public works without including the user fees. Credibility is crucial. The threat of a veto is more or less credible depending upon how badly the president needs the legislation to which provisions, unattractive from his point of view, have been added and upon the president's reputation. President Carter's reputation suffered when he did not carry out his early threat to veto pork-barrel public works.

A Complicated Example

The complexity of strategy at even this stage of the relationship between houses and between Congress and the president is imposing. Still it is intelligible in terms of the general principles and rules. Let me illustrate with an extremely complicated set of events—the unsuccessful effort of President Reagan and other opponents of the Legal Services Corporation to eliminate that organization in 1981. Having failed on that best of occasions, the opponents have not since been able to accomplish their end.

THE SETTING

Federal funding of legal services for the poor has been controversial since it was initiated in the mid-1960s. The system of delivery has always relied primarily on offices staffed with full-time legal services lawyers. Originally funded as part of President Johnson's "War on Poverty," the program has always fought to advance the powers and claims of the poor through litigation. Its opponents might say that the program has emphasized redistribution of wealth through the nonpolitical processes of the courts. The staff attorneys have generally been liberal on economic and social issues, willing to attack both the federal and state governments as well as established economic interests. Some of the earliest and most famous victories of the federally funded programs were over the administration of Governor Ronald Reagan in California in the late 1960s. It is widely accepted that he has opposed the program adamantly since those days.

In 1973 President Nixon and the Congress attempted to neutralize some of the controversy surrounding the funding of legal services by reestablishing the program in the form of the Legal Services Corporation, an organization with a board appointed by the president with the advice and consent of the Senate, a staff appointed by the board, and a substantial annual appropriation of funds to be distributed among legal services offices throughout the country. The opposition did not die down. It grew, and with the incoming conservative tide in the congresses of the late 1970s the demands for abolition or reform became more intense.

By the time President Reagan took office in January 1981 the Legal Services Corporation (LSC) was operating on a continuing resolution because its supporters in the Congress feared they could not pass an authorization and an appropriation. A continuing resolution, like most appropriations, does not last for more than one fiscal year. In his first budget President Reagan recommended no funding for the LSC. Reviewing the president's proposal as part of the extraordinary budget process of his first months in office, a majority of the Senate Labor and Human Resources Committee refused to go along with the recommendation. It recommended and the Senate passed a radically reduced budget for the LSC despite the adamant opposition to *any* funding by the committee chairman, Senator Orrin Hatch, and by the chairman of the relevant subcommittee, Senator Jeremiah Denton.

Such powerful figures can generally have their way when they want to defeat legislation, but on this occasion they were forced to accept the position of a committee majority in order to obtain compensating concessions on a subject of equal concern to them and the president—block grants to the states. But the recommendation of the Senate committee, which was adopted by the full Senate, was scrapped in the unique, not-to-be-repeated 1981 budget conference with the House. The future of the LSC was left to be decided by the normal processes of authorization and appropriation, unaffected by the peculiarities of the budget debate in that first year of the Reagan administration.

Opponents of the Legal Services Corporation, such as the group calling itself the Conservative Caucus, could see that the supporters of legal services, including the American Bar Association, might command a majority in each house, perhaps close to two-thirds. Support would be greatest on any bills reported out of the appropriations process, for the relevant appropriations subcommittees in both houses were chaired by strong supporters of the LSC. Bills attempting to authorize the corporation, which are normally a prerequisite to an appropriation, would have a moderately friendly reception in the House Judiciary Committee. But they would be unlikely ever to find their way through the Senate Committee on Labor and Human Resources, for either Senator Denton or Senator Hatch would be responsible for setting the agenda and both were adamant opponents of the

LSC. They could simply bury the matter, at least unless there was an unusual revolt on the committee. One of the greatest powers of any committee is to decide which proposals to review carefully and to report to the floor, for neither house is anxious to act without a committee recommendation. The chairman of a committee or subcommittee has unusual influence in making this decision.

HOW THE CORPORATION COULD BE RE-FUNDED

Let us look at the matter from the point of view of the Conservative Caucus and of President Reagan's other, governmental lobbyists on the hill. To plan a strategy for eliminating the LSC, they needed to consider the several ways it could be reestablished.

The simplest and most direct way would be for both houses to re-authorize the corporation and then for both houses to appropriate money for it, followed in each case by the president signing the bill. But Senators Hatch and Denton could use their control of the agenda to prevent an authorization from ever reaching the Senate floor. In any event, the president could and would veto any authorization of the LSC if he had to. There was a second way LSC could be kept alive. If the House, where supporters of the LSC chaired the Judiciary Committee and its relevant subcommittee, passed an authorization and then, owing to the efforts of Senators Hatch and Denton, the Senate was unable to consider and pass such a bill, the stalemate might well invite direct recourse to an appropriations bill that disregarded the general rule requiring a prior authorization. The House of Representatives, which takes such matters more seriously than the Senate, would have passed an authorization. The Senate's failure to have passed one would obviously have been attributable to an exercise of the raw powers of a hostile chairman. As I have noted, the appropriations subcommittees that would deal with the Legal Services Corporation were chaired by supporters of the corporation, Senator Lowell Weicker and Congressman Neil Smith. So the Congress might well agree on a bill reestablishing and re-funding the LSC in this way.

The president would find it harder to veto an appropriation bill for LSC, for it would also include funding for the departments of Justice and State. Still, if it arrived on his desk in time for Congress to act again before the fiscal year expired, he might well veto the bill. The veto would be sustained if one-third of either house then voted against the bill, supporting the president's views.

Finally, the conservatives could see that the LSC supporters had a third possibility. Even if the Congress did not pass an authorization or an appropriation, Weicker and Smith might include the Legal Services Corporation in a continuing resolution. That depended, of course, on whether it became necessary to continue the funding of large parts of the federal government in this way at the end of the fiscal year—a necessity that was becoming quite common. It might very well also depend upon whether a continuing resolution was an appropriate way to handle the LSC, because the matter had simply never been reached and finally resolved during the congressional session, or an inappropriate way of attempting to revive a matter that had been already decided contrary to their views with the defeat of a proposed authorization or appropriation. If, for example, an authorization had been defeated by the vote of one house or by a presidential veto, that would have looked like a final and legitimate resolution of the issue, making it far more difficult to find a majority in both houses that would then be willing to take the highly irregular step of including it in either an appropriations bill or a continuing resolution. Many would have thought that the constitutional process had been allowed to work its will and that that will had produced a decision which should now be respected and not immediately reopened.

The conservatives knew that, if the House and the Senate *did* vote to include the LSC in a continuing resolution at the end of the fiscal year, the president would be extremely hesitant to veto it for any reason that was not of obvious national importance. Too many other programs would be disrupted by the veto. Eliminating the Legal Services Corporation was not likely to measure up to that high standard.

TACTICAL CHOICES

Hidden in that complicated set of ways that the Legal Services Corporation could be given new life, there was only one real choice for the opponents of the corporation as they thought about how to use their two primary assets: the resolute support of Senators Hatch and Denton in the Senate committee crucial to authorization—the Committee on Labor and Human Resources—and the prospect of a presidential veto if this were anything but extremely costly to the president. The choice was this. They could, as one option, urge Senators Hatch and Denton to avoid committee and Senate consideration of any proposal to reauthorize the corporation and, only if the senators were overruled by a rebellious majority of their committee members, turn to a presidential veto of the reauthorization and the subsequent fight for a sustaining one-third of the membership of either house. Alternatively, they could urge these powerfully placed and friendly senators to express their views but then allow the matter to get to the floor where it would be duly passed by the Senate. Then the president would happily veto the authorization, as he had promised to do.

The Conservative Caucus and the president's men chose the first path, perhaps on the theory that it gave them one additional string to their bow. They did not take seriously enough the prospect that the supporters of legal services would move directly to an appropriations bill if the Senate committee simply buried a bill that the House had adopted reauthorizing the LSC. In these particular circumstances neither house could be expected to be concerned about the technicalities of requiring an authorizing statute before appropriating funds.

Supporters of the Legal Services Corporation would have all the advantages that flow from sympathetic committees in bringing appropriations bills to the floor. Then the opponents would have to rely on a presidential veto, one that would be more costly to the president than a simple veto of the authorization because the appropriation would include a number of government agencies. Worse, if there were no appropriations action, the same committees supportive of the LSC would bring the matter up as part of the continuing resolution at the end of the year. A veto of this bill would be extremely costly to the president, for the continuing resolution would fund much of the federal government.

What in fact happened was what the opponents of the corporation should have anticipated. After the House had passed a reauthorization by something less than a two-thirds majority, Senators Denton and Hatch buried the authorization bill in their Senate committees. It never reached the Senate floor. Senator Weicker and Representative Smith then predictably attempted to fund the Legal Services Corporation as part of the normal appropriations process. When, as so often happens, that process could not be completed by the end of the year, they shifted their attention and efforts to a continuing resolution. As everyone could have foreseen, a clear majority of each house was willing to continue the funding of LSC as part of this process. The president's choice was then whether to disrupt much of the federal government by vetoing a continuing resolution necessary to keep the government operating after October 1 simply to eliminate the relatively small programs of the LSC. He had other, far higher priorities; the corporation survived.

What if LSC's opponents had chosen the alternative path of urging Senators Denton and Hatch to express their opposition to reauthorization but then to bring the matter to the floor for a full Senate vote? Reauthorization would have passed in the Senate as it had in the House, and after conference the bill would have been sent to the president. President Reagan would have happily vetoed a bill that did nothing else but reauthorize the Legal Services Corporation. A tough fight might well have obtained the necessary one-third of either the Senate or the House of Representatives required to sustain the president's veto.

Once the reauthorization had been vetoed and the veto sustained, it would have been far more difficult to bring the corporation back to life as part of a continuing resolution. Nothing in the rules of either House would have absolutely forbidden it. But some of those who supported the inclusion of LSC funding in a continuing resolution would have thought that step inappropriate had the full constitutional process, involving votes by both houses, conference, veto, and unsuccessful attempt to override the veto, been allowed to work its will. Many in the House and the Senate would have thought that the supporters of the corporation had had their fair chance and had failed.

9 *Legislative Tactics*

Common Concerns of Legislators and Major Choices of Advocates

Beliefs, alliances, interests, and friendships are never wholly separable. That makes it difficult to categorize the concerns of legislators, although that step is necessary to an understanding of legislative tactics. Still, it is important to begin with a reminder of the richness of the mixture, so that what is later left out in cold, analytic categories is less likely to be forgotten.

Legislators are socially and politically located at the intersection of a number of groups, each of which has ties among its members and to the legislator that are cognitive, tactical, interest-based, and emotional. Some of these groups—a very important category—are defined by private constituencies. A representative may self-consciously represent farmers *and* liberals *and* Democrats *and* midwesterners *and* those friends and supporters who sent him or her to the Congress, and so forth. There are also groups in the legislature that claim a particular representative's allegiance, including those based on party, committee, region, and shared views on particular issues of domestic or foreign policy. And there are other more contingent legislative groupings, such as those up for election in the near future or those fearing the electoral results of a particular vote on a weapon or a change in social security benefits.

Each group asks for agreement, loyalty, and tactical cooperation. Yet the demands of the groups are frequently inconsistent with each other.

And, of course, they may be inconsistent with broader notions of what the member owes to the Senate or the House of Representatives, or to the Congress as a whole, or to what he or she sees as the best interest of the nation.

Someone wanting to persuade a legislator would be likely to think and speak in terms of this complex network of loyalties and alliances that both sustain and depend upon the legislator, that offer help and invoke obligations. They represent the substance, the concreteness, that fills the more abstract categories of a representative's concerns. For clarity, I will begin, however, by sketching out those abstract categories, which can then serve as building blocks for a brief introduction to legislative tactics.

FIVE CATEGORIES OF CONCERNS

The first type of factor that may determine a legislator's vote on a proposal is his judgment on its merits. This will reflect his views both of what he thinks is good for the country and of what he believes the constituencies with which he identifies are entitled to on this occasion. His judgments on the merits involve predictions about concrete results; they also turn on what the proposal says about who and what is important to the country and what precedents the action may create. The distinction between the best interest of the nation and obligations to particular constituencies is not of course so precise. Fairness—giving a group or a locale what is its due—is good for the nation too. Beyond that, the legislator's judgment about what the country as a whole needs and what is important to be said to the widest publics and his colleagues about the nation's course may be greatly influenced by the respect or loyalty the legislator feels for the various narrower groups or individuals benefiting or bearing the cost of (and thus, perhaps, arguing for or against) the proposal. We are never free of the pulls of our social alignments on our beliefs.

Second, almost always linked to the first, the member is obviously concerned, crucially in some cases, about what his vote on a proposal will mean in terms of maintaining electoral support. The relationship may be direct in terms of the attention and concerns of particular groups of voters. It may be mediated by the activities or financial support of organized interest groups that can speak to or help the member speak to voters.

The other three factors are more related to loyalties and needs *within* the legislative body. A legislator must consider, third, how her position and actions will affect her influence on other matters, either through changing the chance that others will vote her way or provide other support on some specific piece of legislation or through increasing or reducing her general status or reputation with various powerful individuals or groupings in her house of the legislature. The pressures to support positions important to one's political party are largely explainable in these terms.

Fourth, the member is influenced by what is required for the continued health of the legislative process and of her house and of the Congress as a whole. These depend upon a member giving weight to the needs of a complicated division of labor and to rules for allocating scarce time on a crowded agenda. Legislators feel, for example, that they should defer to the recommendations of a committee that has worked long and hard in developing recommendations. The deference goes beyond the value of its advice and includes a recognition that maintaining concentrated attention in specialized areas requires showing respect, at least when other members are relatively uncommitted on an issue, to the recommendations of a committee that has done the work. More broadly, the fourth concern for process includes doing what is necessary to support and maintain the established system for developing information, making recommendations, allocating scarce time in committee and on the floor, and so forth. In many ways concern for process reflects the member's loyalty to the roles that the legislature and his house play in the governmental system, combined with a recognition that playing those roles well depends upon acceptance of the rules of process.

Finally, legislators are subject to demands of loyalty and friendship. The member will be affected by what he thinks he owes to those who regularly share his views and therefore stand up and support him in a variety of ways, those who work with him as members of his committee and subcommittee, the people at home who vote for him, and his party as well. More personal claims of friendship or prior obligation also belong in this last category.

Any single legislative measure is likely to have an impact along each of these five dimensions. The pressure—and some would say the glory—of the legislator's role often involves the tension of being pulled in different directions by the various implications of a choice. It is even artificial to overemphasize the categories. For example, the demands of loyalty and friendship obviously overlap the other four matters I have listed. One frequently believes on the merits what one's friends believe, worries about the loss of electoral support from taking a position that longtime associates reject, and sees respecting one's colleagues' claims of loyalty as part of the conditions of maintaining influence over other matters. The last is important. The experience of being a legislator often includes prominently the processes of creating and nurturing a network of relations with colleagues not only pleasant but conducive to the necessary give-and-take of legislative choice. Still, loyalty makes its own distinguishable demands as well.

In his splendid account of the passage of an inland waterways bill, T. R. Reid summarizes the most pervasive factors influencing its very complicated "congressional odyssey" as policy, politics, procedure, and personality.* These correspond closely to the five categories I have listed as influencing a member's vote, with my second and third together constituting what he calls politics.

THE EFFORT TO INFLUENCE A MAJORITY OF LEGISLATORS

When a proposal is before the House, scheduled for debate and vote, efforts to persuade require face-to-face contact between uncommitted members and some representative of the sponsors of the proposal (or the opponents) and their various allies. Persuasion will be in terms of all or some of the five concerns or claims that motivate members. Of course the supporters or opponents probably are not thinking in terms as specific to each individual, undecided legislator as, for example, "How does he see this vote affecting his future influence?" They may, but they may think instead of the various groupings the member represents, needs, identifies with, or feels an obligation to. The argument may be in terms of what this means to employment among automobile workers, the hope for safer cars, the recommendations of the committee, and the prospect of a Republican victory in the fall, leaving the uncommitted member to draw the connections among the policies, constituencies, alliances, and obligations mentioned, the groups that shape their relation to him around these matters, and the five concerns I have described.

Less obviously, the arguments available to supporters and opponents when a bill is on the floor depend centrally upon decisions that were made much earlier. I will focus on a set of these that are of unusual importance in winning a legislative battle. The reasons for their importance are straightforward: each of the steps I am about to review affects the reaction of significant groups of members to the proposal (not just the reaction of

*T. R. Reid, *Congressional Odyssey: The Saga of a Senate Bill* (San Francisco: W. H. Freeman, 1980).

single members) and each is likely to be relevant to several of the concerns that ultimately determine the reaction of any member within that group (not just one of those concerns). To understand legislative tactics one must ask particularly what steps will influence a *number* of these factors for *many* members: their view of the merits; their concerns about getting reelected; what they think they will need from others in the governing process; their sense of the needs of process; and their sense of what they owe to friends, colleagues, party, and a variety of supporting constituencies. The answer is that decisions, frequently made quite early, about the design of the proposal, the process through which it will be considered, the occasion when it will be brought up, the legislative allies whose help will be sought, and the private interests involved in the contest play a central role, for they tie intimately into the different claims and concerns of members who will have to vote on the measure.

Let me review the steps in rough chronological order. First there is design. Each of the factors influencing a member's position may be more or less strongly involved, and its very direction of impact may change, depending upon what precisely the proposal says and does. In a legislative contest whoever defines the proposal derives powerful advantages both from being able to specify, in light of predictions as to the concerns of various groups and individuals, what the proposal will and will not do and from being in a position to shape the "face" it holds out (what it says to broad publics) in terms of more widely held beliefs, attitudes, and ideologies.

A second decision of sweeping importance goes to process and particularly the decision as to what committees will handle the proposal. The committee process goes far toward determining what matters will be considered on the floor (in the absence of exceptional efforts by others). The very design of the proposal will be largely determined by the members and leaders of the crucial committees charged with making recommendations. And the decision as to committee allocates the power that comes with expertise and claims to reciprocity and deference in making recommendations to the floor. The fact that any authorization bill for Legal Services would go to the Labor Human Resources Committee in the Senate determines much of what the Senate will do with it. The assignment of the bill to Judiciary in the House may have opposite effects.

Other decisions on process may be almost as important as the choice of committee. Attaching a proposal to a broad budget resolution or a continuing resolution discourages amendments on the floor; it is far easier to amend a separate authorization of, for example, the Legal Services Corporation. Decisions by the Speaker and the Rules Committee (if sustained on the floor) as to what amendments are in order determine the realistic choices available to members and thus, in some cases, the shape of results.

A third broad variable is the choice of exactly when—that is, in what context of other events and salient concerns—a matter is to be brought forth. The party leadership generally sets the agenda for use of the floor. Committee chairmen can delay or advance consideration of matters within their jurisdictions. Whoever can decide on the timing of a proposal may enjoy any number of advantages including: riding a wave of public concern or slipping a matter through when attention is elsewhere, avoiding an overcrowded legislative calendar or forcing a legislative body to address a matter when it feels it has already done enough in that area, having a matter considered in a too obvious association with a similar but unpopular proposal or bringing it up as a matter of simple extension of a popular matter, and so forth. A bill recommending spending to protect our embassies may meet a very different fate depending upon whether or not it is debated in the context of a recent terrorist attack. Indeed matters only marginally related to terrorism are likely to receive a far friendlier reception at that time.

A fourth type of step is the selection and recruitment of allies within the Congress. Some allies—like the senior members of a particular committee or widely respected spokesmen for a viewpoint or well-known protectors of a particular interest or acknowledged experts in a particular specialty— are influential because their views on the merits are assumed by others to be sound or because they have a reputation that provides some protection against electoral attack or, even better, can offer electoral support. Others occupy positions with crucial powers. The chairperson of a committee and the House's leadership can control the conditions of debate, relations with the other house in conference, and some valued perquisites. Party leaders can mobilize party machinery to reach and seek to persuade undecided members; they can provide the help of the president if he is of their party; and they can frequently provide some electoral assistance in advice, endorsement, and money.

The final variable of sweeping importance to the success of a legislative contest is the availability and successful recruitment of private groups organized to influence legislation. In recent years the power of such groups on many matters has rivaled that of the president and the legislative party leadership. Sometimes the path to influence is direct; the member cares about the strongly held views of some interest group. He may simply respect its judgment and admire its leadership. Sometimes the working out of private influence is less direct, operating through the influence of a private group with powerful legislators who in turn can influence others. An organization such as the American Bar Association may be influential with senior Republicans on the Judiciary Committee, who in turn provide needed leadership to still other voting members.

Organized interest or cause groups also have the capacity to use many of their own members or a few paid lobbyists to reach and attempt to persuade a sizable number of legislators or crucially placed committee members with whom they may be influential for any of a number of reasons: their status and reputation; friendship, previous support, or recognized expertise; the support they can furnish on other occasions with other members in the legislative process; or their access to the media and appreciative audiences. Obviously the ability to develop powerful private allies would be a central tactical capacity even if we were to ignore a final influence: the power of private groups to affect future elections. With that power, the role of such allies can be overwhelming.

Well-organized private groups can and do make clear to members that valuable if not crucial help in a campaign (or support for the member's opponent) depends upon support or opposition to a particular legislative proposal. The National Rifle Association contributed hundreds of thousands of dollars to the electoral campaigns of those who later supported the group in its historic and largely successful effort in 1986 to undo gun control legislation. Many believe that what was even more important was the NRA's ability directly to mobilize gun lovers across the country to threaten the reelection of supporters of gun control, an effort supplemented by national media advertising addressed to wider, less committed audiences.

This battle required reaching a substantial majority of the 435 members of Congress. It also required a rich understanding of the process. Neither the Judiciary Committee chairman nor the Speaker of the House of Representatives (some of whose leadership allies supported the NRA) could defeat or even outwit or deflect the NRA on this occasion. Other examples are less dramatic and even commonplace. During the same period, as the Internal Revenue Code was being revised, industry representatives fought to preserve tax advantages by applying more focused financial and other electoral incentives to the far fewer members of the Senate Finance Committee and the House Ways and Means Committee.

Obviously, organized private interests are direct and powerful participants in the legislative process, wielding power in particular cases, like the NRA during the 1986 fight over gun control legislation, far greater than the most powerful members of a house. It can thus be misleading to speak as if politically powerful private interests are merely valuable allies of legislators who have the primary initiative and command responsibility for a legislative proposal and battle. The NRA may, at least as realistically, be thought of as choosing *its* legislative allies for *its* initiative and *its* battle plan.

Most observers believe that, in some overall way, the relative power of strategically placed members and of well-organized interest groups has shifted sharply in the latter's favor with the decline in party influence, the growth of media importance to elections, and the diminution in the formal powers and job security of legislative leaders. But since the importance of each in any particular case will depend upon many factors, we can for simplicity treat even powerful private groups as potential allies, furnishing a final major tactical opportunity and choice to the members pressing or opposing a particular proposal of potential concern to the interest group. The terms *ally* and *opportunity* simply must not be allowed to suggest too secondary a role.

AN EXAMPLE OF MAJOR CHOICES IN ACTION

Let me illustrate the power of these major choices by returning to the battle in 1981 over the continuation of the Legal Services Corporation. The battle for reauthorization was won in the House of Representatives by the supporters of the corporation and lost by the Conservative Caucus and President Reagan. I think the House battle was won by the way the supporters of the Legal Services Corporation handled four of the major choices I have just described—design, process, congressional allies, and private alliances—and by the way their opponents mishandled them.

First, the supporters of the corporation designed their proposal and shaped their arguments in a way far better tailored to meet the concerns of members of the House. The fundamental source of support for the Legal Services Corporation lay in the powerful ideology of respect for an individual's legal rights and the necessity, recognized throughout this century in America, of having legal assistance if one was to enjoy these rights. The strongest argument against the LSC was that its field offices ignored the needs and rights of individuals in order to pursue the social vision and activist agenda of liberal or radical lawyers. Most members would agree that the United States should not fund any private individual's social vision.

The liberal supporters of the Legal Services Corporation dealt with these competing claims partly by arguments and demonstrations that the claims of social activism were greatly exaggerated but, much more importantly, by designing a process and a bill that neutralized these claims. They invited potential opponents to propose statutory prohibitions of anything that even looked like social activism. By reviewing these proposals and then accepting many such restrictions, supporters of the corporation won the support of the uncertain members, whose concerns were carefully considered. And the supporters left as the only remaining issue, after whatever was widely objected to had been prohibited, the right of American citizens to enjoy what is given them by law.

The conservative opposition could have pursued a parallel strategy. They could have developed, as a substitute for the LSC offices with paid staff, an alternative method of meeting individual legal needs. The provision of funding to private practitioners, who had no social agenda, would have served their ends well. Then the legislative contest would have become a choice between meeting legal needs in a traditional, individualistic way or turning the poor over to politicized staff operations. But the opponents of the LSC never designed a comprehensive proposal in this way. Instead they argued implausibly that the states or private attorneys would meet the needs of private individuals without federal reimbursement. And they relied on undocumented claims of social activism despite a process that was incorporating restrictions to deal with whatever reality that problem had and despite the fact that a president sympathetic to their concerns would appoint the governing board.

Although the normal legislative process would have centered on the Democratic majority of the House Judiciary Committee, the corporation's friends modified the process to center instead on the committee's most respected Republican members. Many members of the House would, as always, look to the committee as a whole and particularly to a one-sided vote in the committee for guidance on this controversial issue. But the committee was known to be liberal, far more liberal than the membership of the House as a whole. Conservative members of the House would give great weight to views of the Republicans on the committee, such as Representatives Butler, Sawyer, Railsback, and Hyde. The advocates of the LSC could not expect to win on the floor without their support. Meanwhile the Reagan administration and other opponents of the corporation ignored and slighted these needed allies. Traditionally sympathetic to the argument based on individual rights and responsive to the traditions and status of the American Bar Association, these Republican members of the Judiciary Committee carried the day for the Legal Services Corporation in exchange for being invited to play a leading role in the process of designing the conditions of its reauthorization.

Finally, the liberal supporters of the corporation mobilized the impressive lobbying support of the American Bar Association. A conservative proposal to shift funding to individual practitioners might have divided or immobilized the ABA. An outright attack on the provision of legal services through federal funding simply unified the ABA behind its most encompassing and motivating standard, the need for lawyers if legal rights are to be protected. The ABA brought to the struggle a field operation, a reputation for expert knowledge of legal needs, and a conservative image. Equally important, no substantial lobbying support against the corporation was generated by the conservative opposition.

From Understanding Advantages to Designing Tactics

THE UNEQUAL DISTRIBUTION OF THE CAPACITY TO TAKE ADVANTAGE OF
PROCESS, TIMING, AND ALLIES

The proponents and opponents of the Legal Services Corporation each had central choices to make about design, process, congressional allies, and the use of private groups. It is surprising that choices on timing were not more important. But it would be a serious mistake to fail to recognize that in this case and generally the supporters and opponents of a particular proposal are quite unequally situated with regard to each of the major variables that influence numbers of uncommitted members. Each camp may enjoy relative equality in the choice of the design of its proposal (although within each camp certain members, such as the members of a relevant committee, have much more influence). But in addressing each of the other matters that I have described as central legislative choices, one or the other side has advantages that it can exploit and that its opponent will seek to minimize.

With respect to process—a matter that can be of immense importance—the most important choice concerns the committee that will handle the matter. Often one side will simply enjoy that advantage regardless of any efforts of the other to capture it; for decisions made years ago determine the assignment of many proposals to a particular committee and the membership and leadership of the committee as well. But there is important leeway to draft a proposal so as to direct it to a preferred committee or to have a proposal referred to more than one committee. Action can be taken through the Internal Revenue Code if the taxing committees are preferred to, say, the commerce committees. A bill can be written, without substantive difference, to be a matter for Labor and Human Resources or Finance or Commerce. The resulting difference in process can be determinative. The alternative of changing the leadership and membership of a committee is a difficult and long-range strategy.

Still, both the supporters and opponents of a proposal will generally find that, whatever they do, earlier decisions have determined which side will enjoy the advantages that come from a sympathetic committee and from the committee's capacity to elicit the deference of undecided members in the interest of regularity, expertise, and a desire to maintain a tradition of reciprocal respect for committee recommendations. The side that enjoys this advantage has to fear only rarely that its opposition might successfully divert the proposal into other procedural channels.

Those who control the agenda in a committee or in the House or Senate as a whole usually control the timing when a proposal can be brought forward. The side they favor enjoys some crucial advantages. A widespread public demand for some action in response to a dramatic event or a festering problem may greatly increase the support for any proposal that looks like a plausible answer. Among interest groups and within the legislature itself, what allies will be available to each side depends importantly on the choice of timing for bringing a proposal forward, for the salience of concerns varies at different times depending upon the context of other events and conditions.

Similarly proponents and opponents of a proposal enjoy very different advantages in the other aspects of their ability to recruit allies within the House or Senate, the executive branch, or private groups. The private interests supportive of one side, for example, may already be well organized, attentive, and well financed. The other side may find itself with no such potential for private support. This advantage may be crucial. Allies not only greatly expand the ability to reach large numbers of members. They also invoke the claims of friendship and loyalty, the fears of electoral response, the prospect of bargaining benefits in legislative decisionmaking, and the influence on the merits that comes with trust, ideological sympathy, and expertise.

Supporters and opponents of a particular position are also likely to differ significantly in the ease with which they can identify and communicate with members who might be persuaded to vote their way. Knowing who can be influenced, who has not made up his mind, who will be persuaded by what or by whom, and then using that knowledge may involve substantial practical difficulties. It requires time, energy, and the coordinated activity of a number of individuals in a relatively short period of time. This is the daily work of the party leadership in each house, available to assist those proposals they favor and to resist those they oppose. The capacity to handle these practical difficulties also provides an inherent advantage to: the members of the relevant committee; well-organized lobbying groups; and, more generally, those highly motivated advocates willing to devote unusual amounts of their time and energy to the effort.

All these are advantages in dealing with a number of members simultaneously. There are, of course, also the highly particular advantages that each side enjoys with individual members flowing from a special friendship or antagonism, the good fortune of having control over another bill that matters a great deal to an undecided member, or a particular form of election threat the member faces.

In short, the crucial choices that I have described—design and timing, process, allies—are largely shaped and constrained by the advantages each side has in invoking the steps that would turn that source of influence to its benefit. Each side would like to choose not only the design of a proposal but also the timing of its legislative consideration and the process through which it will proceed. Each side would like to have available the organizational capabilities of private allies and the capacity to know the views of, and communicate with, undecided members. But these are plainly not matters of choice alone. They involve recognition of advantages and disadvantages to each side based on decisions made at some earlier time.

TACTICS AS CHOICES AFFECTING MANY MEMBERS MADE IN LIGHT OF
ADVANTAGES EACH SIDE ENJOYS

The crucial understanding necessary if one is to design legislative tactics is a recognition of the advantages that each side has with respect to the ways that it can reach and call upon the motivations of undecided members. The result of such understanding may be to see that the prospect of success does not justify any substantial investment of time and energy, or it may be the contrary, followed by political action.

Legislative tactics are the choice of actions to exploit one's advantages in reaching and influencing undecided individuals and in maintaining and solidifying support. Tactical choice also involves making it more difficult for the opposition to exploit its advantages. If a proposal that one opposes is a subject of widespread sympathetic concern at a particular time because of a temporary condition or recent events, delay becomes part of the tactics. If delay is unavailable, structuring the crucial choices so that they turn upon procedural votes or highly technical issues again tends to neutralize the advantage of those attempting to ride a tide of popular support. Referral of a matter to two committees may blunt the advantage that would flow from one of the committee's known sympathies for a position you oppose. The variety of possibilities is great.

The simplest way to think about the prospects for a political initiative and about the tactical possibilities that define those prospects is to consider the advantages enjoyed by the supporters and opponents of that initiative.

Designing Tactics in Light of Comparative Advantages: An Example

The political context for consideration of the defense budget in the House of Representatives in 1973 was very similar to the situation a dozen years later in the mid-1980s. The proponents of a dramatic cut in defense expenditures in 1973 included Les Aspin from Wisconsin, a junior congressman on the House Armed Services Committee (who would chair the committee twelve years later). The Republican administration of President Nixon was supporting expansion of defense expenditures at the same time that it was engaged in a confrontation with Congress over the president's refusal to spend funds appropriated for domestic programs. The Congress had voted a total budget ceiling, putting further pressure on any effort to expand a major component of the budget such as defense. Public opinion polls showed majority support for a cut in defense spending. Stories of waste and cost overruns were having their effect then, as they would a dozen years later.

Still, these factors were hardly likely to influence the majority of the House Armed Services Committee. The committee consisted over-whelmingly of congressmen favorably disposed to defense spending. Only the prospect, considered highly unlikely, of a defeat on the floor might force restraint on the committee. Otherwise a substantial majority would vote down Aspin's proposals for cuts in defense expenditures. And if Aspin looked to the prospect of reducing, on the floor, the amount recom-mended by the Armed Services Committee, he would have to anticipate grave difficulties there as well. The deck was stacked in favor of the committee.

THE ADVANTAGES ENJOYED BY THE ARMED SERVICES COMMITTEE

The crucial question was, who and what would persuade representatives when the dispute became a contest between Aspin and the Armed Services Committee? A great majority could be expected to be uncertain on the merits, and many would be relatively unconcerned about public reaction to a routine vote. The committee majority and the House leadership could approach and persuade members far more systematically than Aspin could alone or with a few allies. As for the effectiveness of any approach he could make, Aspin knew that there was a strong disposition to defer to any committee, and particularly the Armed Services Committee, for a number of powerful reasons.

The committee was charged with developing expertise and closely ex-amining the questions that other representatives must address without personal expertise and without much time. Particularly in a technical area, the path of caution suggests deferring to the experts. Other concerns of members would dictate allowing the matter to be decided by the routine procedure that had been established for handling them: a majority vote of the committee. If a representative wants a particular category of matters to be handled in an orderly and intelligent way and sees that a process has been established for delegating responsibility for, and the burdens of, a careful review of these matters, he is likely also to conclude that the system will only work—the necessary attention and time will only be given by those with delegated responsibility—if others follow their lead on most occasions. And Aspin knew that any committee's recommendations were bolstered by the desire of other representatives to see the recommendations of their own committees respected. Finally, most committees, including Armed Services, had specific benefits to offer or withhold if particular votes were badly needed.

These normal advantages of a committee are immensely heightened when the question is providing an adequate defense for the nation. A representative who is uncertain about the underlying issues will not want to find he has helped undermine what may prove to be a crucial defense program, and he will not want his constituents to hold him responsible for that. And any major weapon system involves an array of contracts and subcontracts, funding plants and workers in many congressional districts. Representatives will not vote to cut off a major source of federal funding in their districts. The Armed Services Committee also enjoys the support of massive lobbying efforts by the Department of Defense and defense contractors. The number of supportive experts that can be mobilized is very great.

I should note one final difficulty Aspin faced. To the extent that all these advantages of the Armed Services Committee made it *appear* pointless to contest the committee's recommendations, it would be difficult for Aspin to find allies willing to spend the time and risk the retaliation involved in an attack on the committee. For this reason every committee has a stake in appearing invulnerable by making only recommendations that it can sustain on the floor. That appearance may become a reality just by being taken for granted by potential opponents.

TACTICS AS A WAY OF NEUTRALIZING AN OPPONENT'S ADVANTAGES AND EXPLOITING ONE'S OWN

Aspin succeeded in obtaining a significant reduction (from the Armed Services Committee's recommendation) in the House authorization for defense expenditures; an amendment he offered to the committee's recommendations won on the floor. He enjoyed the advantage of timing; it was an occasion when the media, wider publics, and many representatives from both left and right in the Congress wanted to send a message to the administration and the Pentagon. But he had to overcome his opponents' advantages in terms of process, benefits to constituents, and established executive and private lobbying alliances. Aspin's tactics on this particular occasion are well worth reviewing, for they illustrate clearly the process of designing tactics to exploit or neutralize the advantages of each side.

Aspin had to design a proposal that neutralized the claims of the Armed Services Committee and of the Defense Department to superior expertise; that allayed the fear of representatives and constituents that a necessary weapon system might be foolishly eliminated; and that avoided the threat to employment and profits that comes from canceling a weapon system. Even if he accomplished this, he then had to enlist the help of a body of lobbyists with stakes of their own to match the influence of committee members and their allied Defense Department and industry supporters. If he could do all this, then the determining factor was likely to be what message most members wanted to send—and be seen by constituents as sending—to the Department of Defense: one of unquestioning support or one demanding restraint.

Aspin addressed the problem of design by carefully avoiding an attack on any specific weapon system; instead he proposed an overall ceiling on the total authorization for all weapon systems, set at a level determined by the prior year's appropriation adjusted only for inflation. The Defense Department would be ordered to report back its suggestions for apportioning its reduced budget among weapon systems, giving the Armed Services Committee and Congress thirty days thereafter to review its plan. Unlike an attack on any specific weapon system, the ceiling amendment did not threaten the loss of *specific* jobs or plants and did not represent the assumption by nonexperts of responsibility for crucial decisions about the defense of the United States. The advantages of expert judgment by the Department of Defense and the Armed Services Committee were retained. At the same time the amendment neutralized much of the force of the committee's claim of expert judgment even as to the total authorization, for a total is far harder to defend with specific information furnished by department or private experts than is any particular weapon system.

Aspin dealt with the need for allies by personally convincing members who would be influential—either because of their partisan or policy views (even conservative hawks were dismayed by the apparent indifference of DOD to cost and waste) or because of their committee memberships (for example, members of the Appropriations Committee)—to lend their reputation and sometimes their energies in making contact with other members. He also persuaded some well-organized interest groups concerned with domestic programs that, in a year when there was an overall budget ceiling, their own interests demanded that defense spending be limited. The coalition included groups such as the U.S. Conference of Mayors, the National Association of Home Builders, the National Education Association, and the United Mine Workers. Allies are not, however, a substitute for personal effort. Aspin devoted an immense amount of personal time to his own contacts with other members. His amendment passed the House by a 242–163 vote.

Of course, as we have seen, a victory in one house is only part of the game of legislative politics. Broader tactics require recognizing that there is more than one legislative occasion for addressing a matter and also planning for action in more than a single house of Congress. On this occasion Aspin gave little attention to this.

In actual fact, a relatively small reduction in the authorized ceiling for defense systems was not likely to make any difference. For one thing, the appropriations decision generally controls the amount of defense spending; it regularly cuts well beneath the amount authorized and in this case it even cut well below the amount Aspin would have authorized. Moreover even the authorization was not really cut, for the supporters of defense spending had other cards to play. Aspin should have foreseen that, when the House and Senate defense authorization bills came to conference, a majority of the conferees representing the House would be supporters of the committee position. They are picked by the Speaker of the House on advice of the chairman of the committee that worked on the bill. If there was no Senate equivalent of Aspin's amendment—and there was not—the House conferees would simply agree to adopt the Senate position, which was much closer to their own views on this matter. And this is what they did.

It took remarkable skill to win as much as Aspin won. But really to accomplish something he would have had either to devise a similar plan in the Senate or to bring the House to take the very unusual step of instructing its conferees not to give in on the Aspin amendment. And he would have had to impose a ceiling so low that it had some effect on the appropriations bill.

The Long-Run Strategy of Building Advantages

Advantages in policy battles can be created for the future as well as used on a particular occasion. The management of politics involves going beyond tactics and a particular case to the marshaling of advantages for a particular person or committee or interest group and to the creation of the conditions under which particular types of proposals will themselves have an advantage over time. The management of politics is the pursuit of wholesale and lasting advantages for one's self, one's organization, and one's policies. In the two chapters that follow I will refer to the advantages that flow to individuals and organizations as "resources" and those that flow to particular proposals as matters of the "setting" for political choice.

The management of politics involves attending to the long run. It relates to the tactics of legislative politics as wisdom relates to cleverness. A clever tactical plan can bring about legislated results on a particular occasion. But effective managers of politics will have their way on many more occasions, losing occasional battles but winning a larger war.

THE REAL STAKES IN ASPIN'S EFFORT

Thus it is a serious mistake to be distracted by victories won with well-considered and clever tactics. In 1973 Aspin won only part of a single battle, not a war. Aspin was opposing a relatively ineffective chairman. He had the advantage of unusually favorable timing and surprise. Even with all this, his victory had no apparent policy effects.

This may be a little unfair. If so, it is important to see why. What was really at stake here was the prospect of change in the setting for future decisions about defense spending, in particular the influence of the House Armed Services Committee, its chairman, F. Edward Hebert, and Congressman Aspin.

If the committee was to be influential in important defense decisions, it had to win on the floor. It was far more likely to win if it had a reputation for being almost invulnerable. Aspin damaged that reputation. If the committee was to be important to other members who wanted something from the Department of Defense, and to the Department of Defense when it wanted something from the Congress, the executive branch had to consider the committee a very powerful, almost controlling influence in the House on questions within its jurisdiction. That too depended upon its winning regularly. Here it lost dramatically.

If Chairman Hebert was to lead the committee, he had to show that he could protect its stake in winning. Aspin damaged Hebert's position in the committee. At the same time, Aspin strengthened his own position in the committee and in the House. He would find it easier to mount a floor attack on the committee's recommendations in the future. Knowing that, the members of the committee would have to pay more attention to him in committee deliberations.

There are more than personalities and committees involved. What I have just said could have been expressed as easily in terms of two sides in a debate about the level of defense expenditures. Because of its stakes in winning, the committee henceforth had to be more cautious in addressing the issue of defense expenditures. Aspin's victory showed the potential power of any members (not just Aspin) who were willing to push the cause of budgetary restraint at a time of public skepticism about defense expenditures. Hebert's position on these issues also had to change as he looked for more secure ground. The setting facing defense expenditure proposals had thus shifted in the direction of better prospects for restraint in expenditures.

THE LONG-TERM ADVANTAGES NEVER REALLY CHALLENGED BY ASPIN'S EFFORTS

But how much had resources and setting changed? I think very little. Aspin's victory and whatever shifts in resources and setting it brought about were largely distractions from a far more important, far more stable picture. Membership on the Armed Services Committee still went largely to those who had bases or plants in their districts or had unusually strong views and constituencies favoring military spending. The capacity of the Department of Defense to furnish assistance in a variety of ways to the members of the committee would continue to bolster this policy leaning.

Together the Department of Defense and the committee continued largely to monopolize the expertise necessary for intelligent decisions on complicated weapon systems or basing patterns. Together they could still control the location of contracts and bases with the great influence this provided. Together, and assisted by industry lobbyists, they could regularly reach more members with their persuasive message than any likely opposing coalition or position could. With these assets the chairman could produce a committee position that would win on the floor, although it was largely uncritical of defense spending. He would still be bolstered in this by the procedural advantages that every committee chairman enjoys in floor debate and in conference. With a clever plan and a lot of energy a dissenter might win an occasional battle on an auspicious occasion, but the forces of those supportive of defense spending remained overwhelming in the long run. Relatively major changes would have to wait for another decade.

Management of politics is understanding and handling the forces that assemble a strong hand for the long-term support of particular policy positions or for the accumulation of personal or organizational political resources. The strength of the prodefense position on weapons acquisition has not been an accident. It is intelligently and carefully managed. A combination of crucial advantages—a particular system for selecting committee members, the control of information, the placing of contracts and bases, the marshaling of lobbying resources, the use of public information and support, and an ability to exploit favorable timing—creates a hand that wins regularly and discourages opposition.

These are the high stakes of politics. Tactics, with its fascination and diversity, is a game played in the shadow of the management of politics.

10 The Meaning of "Resources" in a Political Setting

In discussing Aspin's effort to cut defense expenditures in 1973 I have emphasized the advantages that either an individual or a particular policy may enjoy in a legislative debate. But it is useful to distinguish the advantages held by an individual, his *resources* of influence, from the advantages enjoyed by a particular policy, which depend more broadly on the *setting* for decision. This chapter will deal with resources; the chapter that follows, with setting. While examining the resources of both executive and legislative officials and policy debates within the executive branch as well as in Congress, I will emphasize legislative resources, for these are less obvious.

By an individual's *resources* I mean whatever makes it possible to influence the response of other legislative or executive officials to a proposal. Resources describe a relationship between defined parties. The secretary of defense has many resources with regard to millions of individuals, but he may have little capacity to affect the actions of a postal clerk; and he may be less important to a middle-level staff employee of the Appropriations Committee than the latter is to him.

Some illustrations will help clarify what I mean. Let us first take a look at the influence of Congressman Aspin ten years later, in 1983, as he lends crucial support to President Reagan's effort to obtain an MX strategic missile. Since Aspin was not yet chairman of the Armed Services Committee, this episode provides a useful vehicle for exploring the informal bases of influence. Then, we will look back at the enormous advantages enjoyed by one of the most powerful of chairmen, Representative Wilbur Mills, when he was chairman of the House Ways and Means Committee.

An Example: The Fight for the MX

Brevity requires taking some serious risks of oversimplification in describing the battle over the MX missile in 1983. In the late 1970s it began to appear that Soviet intercontinental ballistic missiles (ICBMs) were becoming numerous and accurate enough to eliminate most American land-based missiles in their silos. The United States had submarines and bombers to respond to a first-strike attack against land-based missiles, but for some time national strategy has been based on maintaining three independent forces, each capable of retaliation *after* a first strike. Moreover the very capacity to hit the rival's missiles and destroy them, if enjoyed only by the Soviet Union, might create political advantages in international intimidation.

First President Carter and then President Reagan proposed building a new, more powerful, and more accurate American missile, the MX. Each president considered a variety of systems for basing the new missile in such a way that it could survive a Soviet first strike. But none of these basing modes could plausibly be said to be likely to enable the MX to survive a Soviet attack. In late 1982 Congress gave the president only one more chance to come up with a policy on basing the MX; if he failed, construction of the missile would not be funded. The conservatives in both houses were concerned about the obvious strategic weakness of a plan that did not involve a safe location for the missiles. Liberals were more concerned about arms control and inflamed by the hardline positions taken by Reagan administration officials such as Assistant Secretary of Defense for International Security Affairs Richard Perle.

President Reagan impaneled a prestigious commission chaired by retired air force general Brent Scowcroft and asked it to examine all the questions surrounding strategic, intercontinental missiles. Key members of the Scowcroft Commission, seeing that the question was as much a matter of politics as military strategy, quickly made contact with Congressman Les Aspin who, by the early 1980s, had developed a reputation for skepticism, intelligence, and reliability that led a number of people in the House to follow his vote on defense matters.

Aspin thought the MX missile could not be killed permanently by Congress, and he believed that the effort to do so would only hurt the Democratic party and, more important, destroy any chance that the administration would bargain seriously about arms control with the Soviet Union. He was therefore willing to negotiate with the commission and, through it, with the Reagan administration. The Scowcroft Commission, consulting with Aspin, produced a report that favored the MX, as President Reagan very much wanted. But the commission also urged a shift in strategic emphasis from large multiwarhead missiles like the MX to far more numerous, smaller missiles ("Midgetmen"), many of which, because of their greater total numbers, would be likely to survive attack and which could more easily be made the subject of arms control negotiations. Finally, the commission endorsed certain crucial changes in the administration's negotiating positions on arms control agreements. Both of the latter recommendations were much favored by liberal opponents of the Reagan nuclear strategies.

While recognizing explicitly that the MX missile could not be based in such a way that it would be safe against Soviet attack, the Scowcroft Commission argued that it was necessary for a variety of diplomatic and negotiating, as well as military, reasons. But these arguments alone would not win a majority in the House of Representatives; the commission and the president needed the help of members generally opposed to the MX missile but strongly favoring the arms control measures also recommended by the Scowcroft Commission. Thus the objective of the Reagan administration was to provide enough assurance of its good faith on arms control to win the support of Aspin and a few others influential in the House who could deliver votes for the MX missile at a time when the public was much concerned about the nuclear arms race. Because of House rules, there could be no amendment to the simple proposal that the MX missiles be funded. In any event, one could not write arms control measures into the statute. So Aspin and his associates, calling themselves "the working group," demanded a letter from President Reagan promising to proceed on the non-MX recommendations of the Scowcroft Commission. The president's response was encouraging in tone but vague in specifics.

Still, recognizing that a major new weapon system like the MX must receive new authorizations and new appropriations each year, the working group was satisfied that it could threaten to end the program if the Reagan administration did not change its negotiating positions on arms control and also go forward with the smaller, more stable missile (Midgetman) favored, for arms control reasons, by the working group. They recast the crucial vote in the House of Representatives as one in which supporters of arms control should vote for the MX missile in order to change President Reagan's positions on arms control. Then, along with members of the Scowcroft Commission, the working group lobbied actively among potential swing voters, carrying enough who trusted their judgments to win for the MX missile, 239–186. The battle had to be repeated again and again in the years that followed.

The Basic Conditions of Influence

With this story as background, we can review the basic conditions of influence in a contest for votes or for a favorable decision in the executive branch. I will start by considering the several ways that one player can affect the choice of actions by another. There are basically five: authority, persuasion, bargaining, appeal to the need for coordinating leadership, and personal relationships. I can then identify the types of resources needed for successfully using each method of influence.

I. AUTHORITY
Any player can, within limits, take it for granted that another player will regard an authoritative decision or order of his superior as a directive from which he is not free to depart. The arms control negotiators in Geneva must obey the president. It is possible, however, to exaggerate the importance of authoritative directions. Very few orders are so specific that they do not allow discretion; as Lieutenant Colonel North demonstrated vividly, ambiguity alone leaves room for choice. Even when the directive is clear, much may depend on the attitude of the subordinate to the superior and to orderly process within a bureaucracy. If the subordinate questions the motivations and wisdom of the superior and doubts the importance of reliable action in this case, only the chance of detection and the prospect of sanctions will cause him to follow the directive. The military services, for example, did not feel called upon to remove strategic missiles from their bases in Turkey at the direction of President Kennedy. Nonetheless, the authority of a superior position remains a powerful form of influence.

Other authoritative rules can be just as binding as the claims of hierarchy. The clearest examples involve legislative or constitutional mandates. Anyone can invoke, even with a president, a constitutional rule or a statute that seems to mandate or forbid a particular action in a specific situation. President Nixon's powers to make war in Indochina were restricted by statute; the same was true of President Reagan's powers in Central America. If the law is moderately clear, officials cannot afford to ignore it. Public and congressional attitudes toward violations of the law are so certain and so infused with the prospect of political sanctions that rarely can a legal duty be openly avoided. In the early 1980s, for example, the Department of Defense could not seriously consider spending any funds for the MX missile unless it could show this to be consistent with the intent of its authorizations and appropriations.

The courts play a special role in the area of legal authority. A judicial decision forbidding or requiring some form of administrative action provides a powerful inducement even if there is no threat of judicial sanctions. Nixon delivered the Watergate tapes, although the courts had no armies. In a closely related way, the authorized executive branch interpreter of legal rules shares the influence of those whose positions permit promulgation of such directives. Lawyers in government often claim an expertness in, and enjoy the prerogative of, interpretation of judicial decisions, statutes, and the Constitution. Thus the general counsel of a department has authority over its head when the lawyer can argue convincingly that an action is legally forbidden or required.

One final form of authority deserves mention. When a role in government decisionmaking is played by a group or individual too busy to decide for itself or himself what matters to attend to, consider, and act upon, someone else must be given the authority to set the agenda. A person authorized to determine what proposals others shall consider can obviously affect their decisions by denying them the opportunity to act on certain matters. Someone must control the agenda of the House Armed Services Committee, and with that control (largely in the hands of the chairman) goes the power to prevent committee consideration of some matters. The Rules Committee can, and does, recommend that certain bills shall not be subject to amendment or shall be subject to only certain amendments on the floor. In routinely accepting such recommendations, the House denies itself the right to consider alternatives.

2. PERSUASION

A player is seldom certain how he should respond to a particular proposal. The relationship of the proposal to his views of the national interest is often obscure both because he does not possess determinative facts and because understanding the relationship of any facts to his views may require more time, skill, and effort than he has available. The impact of the proposal on interested constituent groups or on his organization may be unclear. Even his personal stakes in acquiescence or refusal are frequently hard to decipher. Needing help with each of these questions, a player needs and invites the help of others whom he trusts and who can provide facts and analysis or simply conclusions. Persuasion is thus a second general way to influence the response of other players. It requires a number of resources.

To start with, persuasion requires access to the player. Access, in turn, can be based on organizational position, on friendship or having provided past support, on the needs of cooperative interaction in this or other situations, on a recognized congruity of attitudes and beliefs, on reputation for knowledge in the area or soundness of analysis or conclusions, and surely on other bases as well. Access is a crucial resource, cannot be taken for granted, can be broadened and deepened over time. Near the core of the gains hoped for by Aspin and the working group in exchange for their support of a costly weapon they thought unwise was continuing access to top-level administration decisionmakers dealing with strategic weapon systems and arms control.

The importance of access as a resource is recognized in the rules that prohibit its use in certain circumstances. A subordinate (for example, someone working for Richard Perle, assistant secretary of defense) cannot ask for direct access to a superior (the secretary of defense) of his immediate superior (Perle) except in unusual circumstances. Similarly, a bureaucratic player is generally expected not to seek access to interested publics or legislators in an effort to influence his bureaucratic superiors. Presidents have fired even cabinet officers for this. Carried out in secret by subordinates, the practice of seeking such forbidden access by "leaking" information has tormented every recent president.

Granting access is costly for a time-pressed player. High-level officials can afford neither the time to hear and resolve all matters others would like them to act upon nor even the time to decide what matters they should resolve. Thus, as I have noted, they need and use staff resources to determine what matters they should and should not attend to and when. Since the authority to decide who will enjoy what opportunity for persuasion, and when, is itself an important determinant of government action, those who are given this authority by busy officials are given a major bargaining resource.

Access is necessary but not sufficient for an exercise of influence through persuasion. Some measure of trust in the player's honesty is also necessary, and this often requires a reputation built up over time. It also requires a conviction that the adviser has no undisclosed self-interest in the action he is urging—a form of trust that was hard for Aspin to enjoy so long as his powerful, central role in the MX debate seemed a possible path to higher positions.

Nor is honesty enough. Without a reputation for having a special knowledge of the relevant facts, a more general expertness in the area, or at least an unusual ability to analyze and clarify the issues in terms of the other persons's beliefs and attitudes, a player has little to offer others in the way of help. Aspin's influence with a number of representatives who listen to his views on defense matters depends upon maintaining such a reputation.

If access and credibility are assured, the capacity, often attributable to loyal and competent staff resources, to develop and analyze the facts relevant to a policy question more intelligently and completely than other players will, without more, control outcomes. Thus Weinberger, Perle, and the chairs of pertinent House and Senate committees and subcommittees—each of whom controls an expert and loyal staff—enjoy a substantial advantage over other players in the defense arena. The absence of comparable staff resources for dealing with weapon issues constitutes a notable weakness of the Department of State in this area.

Even with one or more of these resources, the party seeking to persuade will find his influence limited if he does not know, or is not able to show that he knows, the likely reactions of other players important to the person he is trying to influence, and if he does not know the personal, political, and organizational impact on that person of what he is proposing. Aspin had to understand the political needs of Democrats from the South and of others from New England if he hoped to plan a course of action on the MX for the House or its Democratic members. Knowledge of what the proposal is likely to mean to other players is still another crucial resource that can be developed over time.

Finally, the part of trust that goes beyond a reputation for honesty and is based on either an unquestioned loyalty to the other player's self-interest or a substantial congruence of stakes with respect to a proposal is a resource that can be sufficient to determine the response of the other player if he is busy with other matters. A number of members of the House had this feeling about Aspin in the defense area. The fear that President Reagan had given such a blank check of trust to his hardliners on arms control motivated Aspin and the working group in their effort to strengthen their own access and that of the administration moderates.

3. BARGAINING

Players can and do exercise influence upon each other's actions without reliance on authority or the capacity to persuade. One of the principal remaining devices is the implicit or explicit promise of benefit or threat of harm that is often available to one or more players. In the case of the MX fight of 1983, Aspin and the working group could promise to deliver or withhold thirty or forty votes on the missile President Reagan wanted, depending on the president's willingness to take other actions he did not endorse or favor. But this example is obvious and familiar. Other types of bargaining assets are almost too varied for description, for they represent the control of any private or public resources that can meet or frustrate any of the needs of other political actors for accomplishing goals, building influence, or maintaining and improving their positions.

The president's staff, for example, controls access to the president that is needed for a persuasive effort to affect his use of authority. A determined committee chairman can block or delay legislation wanted by the president; and the president can campaign in, and direct federal expenditures or campaign aid to or from, the legislator's state or district. One executive branch official can assist another in difficult circumstances or he can refuse. An interest group with a stake in MX construction can help or hurt a congressman or his opponent in the next election.

Not far beneath the surface of any discussion between political players lies a shared recognition of the capacity of each to affect directly or indirectly what is important to the other's views of his personal welfare or that of his organization, groups important to him, or the nation. But a player's capacity alone does not shape the decisions of others. They must and will also consider the likelihood that the player will use the resources available to him to reciprocate, with benefits or interference, their helpful or harmful actions. Reputation with regard to bargaining determination and style is a distinct resource that combines with capacity to give influence. Rarely are such considerations made explicit or related directly to a particular proposal, but they always influence the context of relationships over time, going far toward defining the deference that will be paid to the views and wishes of a player.

4. CENTRALITY

A fourth method of influence is closely related to authority and persuasion. Occupying a central position—a natural center for coordination—in any area in which governmental or organizational policy would obviously be harmfully fragmented in the absence of voluntary deference to the lead of a single responsible actor or organization is an important source of influence. The sensed need for national unity and consistency in national defense creates a far heavier presumption in Congress in favor of the president's views on major strategic issues than on domestic issues. The need and the presumption are greatest at the time of great power negotiations. The need for a single voice in such negotiations requires even the president to give discretion to the centrally located negotiators. But, again, the concept is far more general than these dramatic examples.

The obligatory force that players attribute to directives of a bureaucratic superior is largely habitual, socially or organizationally reinforced, and unconsidered. In part, however, it is based on the legitimacy that flows from a recognition that only a coordinated effort can be truly effective in any policy area and that the superior is better situated to provide the necessary coordination by virtue of her broader view of relevant concerns and her clearer accountability to elected, ultimately responsible superiors. In many situations players who are not hierarchic superiors of those they wish to influence can nonetheless invoke the same claims of legitimacy.

Thus the force of claims based on the centrality of a particular official's responsibilities with regard to a particular issue carries over with significant effects to relations among peers. Much of the influence on the floor of the House Armed Services Committee may flow from its claim to deeper understanding of the matters within its jurisdiction. But a committee often receives additional deference, even by those who are unpersuaded by the members' expertness, because others recognize the benefits of consistent and coordinated actions and of centralized accountability in an area such as defense. The same is true for executive branch officials with daily responsibility for a program. Moreover, a committee (or an official) can be expected to fight to maintain its reputation for competence and control with regard to matters central to its jurisdiction. The two effects are complementary. The personal stakes warn that, in areas of his central responsibility, a player will not easily give in to the views of others. At the same time arguments based on the wisdom of deference to whatever organization or committee is best situated to provide badly needed coordination, consistency, and accountability suggest a sensible and face-saving basis for resolving policy disputes.

Centrality as a source of influence comes into play in two different contexts: in terms of who speaks authoritatively as to the impact of a proposal on particular concerns and in terms of whose views carry the most weight when differing concerns suggest different government actions. The former was powerfully illustrated in the MX case in 1982. Congress had asked the Joint Chiefs of Staff to comment on a particular basing plan put forward by their civilian superiors in the Reagan administration for protecting the MX missile against Soviet attack. The skepticism of a clear majority of the Joint Chiefs carried the full weight of their central responsibility for fighting wars. Their dissenting views on the crucial issues of survivability and feasibility predictably killed the proposal of the Secretary of Defense.

Equally important is the effect of centrality when differing concerns compete to control choice. No one short of the president is a common superior of the assistant secretary of defense for international security affairs and the assistant secretary of state for political-military affairs, whose responsibilities overlap and whose views frequently differ. One may look at arms sales in terms of defense needs; the other, in terms of relations with other nations. A disagreement about most matters will not be worth the president's time and it is likely to be beyond his technical competence. In this situation, one player or organization must defer to another or bear the costs of forcing a dispute on major cabinet-level officers, often about a matter that should not occupy their time.

If both parties, though disagreeing on the merits, can see that each has a reasonable position, it is often natural to defer to the one whose jurisdiction includes formal responsibility for routinely deciding similar matters in the absence of any objection from the other. If that in turn is uncertain, the dispute is likely to be resolved by giving jurisdiction to the party whose regular operating responsibilities are more directly involved and in danger of disruption. The assignment of jurisdiction over a matter to a particular committee by the parliamentarian in the House is crucial in determining the power of competing legislative committees, and this too is a decision made in terms of the relationship of the matter to the central operating responsibilities of the various contenders. The committee that routinely processes similar matters can more credibly claim the right to handle the proposed legislation, with extremely important consequences for the ultimate outcome.

5. RECIPROCITY AND LOYALTY

Not every proposal is assessed in terms of its consequences for the player, his organization, or his view of societal needs; and few are assessed completely in such a calculating way. Government players, like everyone else, obtain much of their joy in life and work, their self-esteem, and their sense of community from cooperative relationships with others. Recognition of the claims of reciprocity and loyalty is the condition of being and feeling oneself a member of a team. When a valued coworker, friend, or ally approaches with a proposal, the valued relationship may provide not only access but cooperation, at least in that high proportion of cases where not much else turns for the player on his choice of position with regard to the proposal. Thus, being in a relationship where one can assert claims of reciprocity and loyalty is itself an important resource of influence. Having done favors for or shown loyalty to another creates obligations that are resources.

The purely personal quickly becomes merged with long-term working relationships which dictate cooperative reactions for reasons that relate to the future as well as the past. Superiors often exchange trust for the personal loyalty of immediate subordinates in a context of friendship. The resulting relationship creates felt obligations on the part of each to further the purposes of the other. Players with interlocking interests or with common views of the national interest become friends as they recognize the benefits of standing together on any proposal that one feels strongly about and the other does not. In effect, they have formed an alliance that creates influence for each with the other.

Much depends on whether the policy area has become a recognized battlefield of competing interests or is generally felt to be an area of rational pursuit by government colleagues of widely shared values. If the understanding is that competition is unrestrained and the stakes are high, the demands of loyalty to allies in any contest with opponents are great. This was the feeling among the camps of those supporting and opposing the MX missile. Because the opponents had long regarded Aspin as an ally, his successful leadership in President Reagan's effort to authorize construction of the MX in 1983 created deep resentments. In a different context—if there is not unrestrained competition but an understanding that all are working together to find a sensible means to accomplish shared ends—friends and allies will be under far less pressure to accept particular policy positions, both because the policy skeptics are also owed consideration and because long-term alliances are far less important.

The Importance of the Configuration of Resources

So far I have reviewed the atomic particles of political influence. But it is not the *total* of claims and resources that matters. It is their *configuration*—that is, their allocation and distribution—as they relate to particular issues and as these issues relate to other matters of importance to various political actors. To understand what the configuration of resources means, it is helpful to turn to the position of the chairman of a powerful committee. By the time Aspin became chairman of the Armed Services Committee in 1985 the powers of chairmen, and particularly of one of the most powerful of all congressional chairmen, the chairman of the House Ways and Means Committee, had been substantially reduced by a series of rule changes in the early 1970s. The clearest way to explain the importance of the configuration of resources is to return to the late 1960s and look at the power of the extremely talented, longtime chairman of the House Ways and Means Committee, Wilbur Mills.

Wilbur Mills was central to the creation of medicare and medicaid and was powerful in matters of foreign trade. But it is convenient to focus on another area, tax policy. There his power flowed from the extent to which he monopolized crucial resources to influence the Ways and Means Committee, and from the extent to which the Ways and Means Committee, in turn, monopolized control of resources affecting tax policy in the House of Representatives. I begin with the latter.

What was and is the source of the Ways and Means Committee's influence on tax policy in the House? Tax decisions are generally technical; understanding them requires time that few representatives are prepared to spend. The committee has a monopoly on expertise in the area, supported importantly by a thoroughly professional, sizable staff operation. Its tax recommendations are usually reported to the floor under a rule that forbids or sharply limits amendments. To defeat a proposal on the floor in the face of a closed rule (forbidding all amendments), an opponent would not only have to convince others that he knew better than the committee but also that it was wiser to do nothing at all than to adopt the committee's recommendations. The committee has powerful bargaining assets: it can do important favors for other members when their constituents need help on tax matters; and other parts of its jurisdiction—social security, welfare, international trade, and so forth—are equally important to other members.

In the late 1960s, at the time of Chairman Mills, there was still another great power: the Democratic members of Ways and Means also served as the Democratic Committee on Committees making the all-important assignments to committees that would determine the influence that other members would have for years to come. And the committee's image helped. To attack successfully a recommendation of the Ways and Means Committee, an opponent would have to convince many other representatives that there was a chance of winning. But the committee's expertise and its bargaining assets were enough to make this unlikely, and its care in bringing to the floor only matters on which it was quite certain to win created a reputation for invincibility that discouraged challenges. Even the president could not mount an effective attack on the committee's recommendations. The risks for him were great. The executive branch did not have superior expertise, and the House recognized that it enjoyed the central responsibility in the tax area (unlike, for example, the area of national defense).

In sum, it was the configuration of resources on tax matters—the areas of monopoly of the atomic particles of influence—and the reputation for winning, which reflected that configuration, that made the Ways and Means Committee so powerful. That others lacked the resources necessary for an effective challenge was equally crucial.

The configuration of resources *within* a legislative or bureaucratic unit is also the key to power there. In bureaucratic units, resources are concentrated in the hands of bureaucratic superiors. There is obviously the claim of legitimacy that goes with hierarchical position, that is, authority. Claims to centrality where coordination is needed subtly bolster the influence of superiors. Beyond this, a bureaucratic superior has available the bargaining influence over the other members of the unit which comes with the right to control many of the conditions that are important to the concerns of its members in such a way as to reward cooperation. In a bureaucracy the rewards of salary, power, status, convenience, access, and so forth are obviously possibilities, though often there are legal limits on their use. And using them depends upon having adequate information on whether the conditions for rewards or sanctions have occurred—no easy matter in many cases.

Obviously in a committee, where authority over ultimate choice is vested in the majority, bargaining assets bear a greater role. But consider the powers of any committee chairman in the House of Representatives until the late 1960s. He could set the agenda determining what matters the committee would deal with, could create subcommittees and assign members to them, assign matters to subcommittees of his choice, allocate staff, control the time allotted to members at hearings. and allocate travel funds. He could share or monopolize credit for the work of the committee. Equally important, the members of the committee had no offsetting bargaining power, for the chairman's position and the bargaining assets that went with it were an accepted right of seniority. A reputation for being willing to use these bargaining assets could go far toward providing massive control of the committee's work.

Specifically, Wilbur Mills's power sprang from his ability to influence a committee that was itself so influential on the floor of the House. Among the committee members, he had the greatest knowledge in the tax area and the closest relations to an expert staff. Many of his colleagues were uninterested in this technical area and thus all the more willing to support him. He controlled the agenda of the committee, created no subcommittees (which might make their own claims on the agenda or pose as rival sources of expertness), and established procedures for recognizing the private bills that committee members needed for their own constituents or wanted in order to preserve their influence with other representatives. He was the leading conferee when the House and the Senate met to resolve differences.

A Reputation for Winning

In one sense the reputation that grows out of being favorably situated in the configuration of resources surrounding a particular policy area is simply a restatement of that advantage. One who looked at Wilbur Mills's resources in the late 1960s would recognize that they were considerable. But there is an independent force that comes from a reputation for winning; it works in two ways.

A successful challenge to Mills's views in the committee or to the committee's view on the floor would require the cooperative actions of many other players. But the challenge would be costly for them and would not be undertaken unless the prospects for success were good. Challenging a player with a reputation for controlling the actions of a committee or of the House in a particular area is almost by definition a discouraging prospect. The supporters whom the challenger needs are not anxious to waste their time and energy, let alone incur the risk of retaliation, unless the prospects for success are substantial. Even then it would have to be a matter of unusual importance, for the powerful player being challenged might well remember and retaliate on a later occasion.

The prospects for successful challenge are bad if the player, like Wilbur Mills or his committee, has a reputation for winning. The reputation has an independent force, magnifying the resources at the player's disposal; for it not only reflects the player's capabilities and resources but also reduces the chances of assembling an adequate countervailing force. Mills and the other members of the Ways and Means Committee recognized this. They would go to some lengths to assure that they were not found on the losing side in a policy debate within their jurisdiction.

There is a second aspect of a reputation for winning, and it too has an independent force. Consider, for example, the effect of Mills's reputation for control in the Ways and Means Committee. It meant that powerful actors outside the unit—even the president of the United States—would come to him when they needed the committee's support; seeing that, members of the committee and members of the House at large would turn to Mills when they needed help in dealing with powerful outside figures who owed Mills favors or might need his help. As a center of brokerage, a player with a reputation for winning can multiply his effectiveness by charging a reasonable brokerage fee. By using his support on matters about which he cares less, he can win his way on matters that are more important to him.

The same two effects of reputation are also at work within the executive branch. If Richard Perle has a reputation for winning the support of Secretary of Defense Weinberger when he is challenged by peers in the Defense Department or if the secretary of defense has a reputation for winning the support of President Reagan when other cabinet members disagree with him or his department, challenges are discouraged.

Similarly, considerations of reputation for winning shape the political strategies of Treasury officials with authority to write regulations in the tax area. In response to the initiative of its tax committees, Congress can overrule tax regulations by a change in the statute; and courts can reject Treasury regulations as inconsistent with the statute. Each of these actions will be more readily undertaken—and invited by taxpayers—if the prospects of success look promising. Therefore, the responsible officials of the Treasury Department take care to build and maintain a reputation for not being overruled in their interpretation of the Internal Revenue Code. The reputation for success becomes an independent asset, discouraging others from undertaking the costs of challenge.

The other aspect of a reputation for winning—the brokerage function that it permits—is important in a bureaucracy, although it is often less obvious. If the assistant secretary of treasury for tax policy enjoys a reputation for influence within Treasury in dealing with questions about the interpretation and application of the Internal Revenue Code, legislators will come to him for administrative actions; executive branch officials will then turn to him to deal with those legislators on a later occasion. And an interest group that wants a regulatory or statutory change in the provisions for handling its tax problems may prove useful later on different matters important to Treasury.

Even the influence of a bureaucratic superior with his subordinates is affected by this form of reputation. The ability to get his organization to do what he wants makes the leader important to powerful outside actors; his influence with outside actors makes the benefits of following his leadership greater for his subordinates and the prospects of challenging it less promising.

Leadership in an Organized Unit

An individual's power or influence often works through his ability to control the activities of an office or committee that is itself influential because of its position in the configuration of resources surrounding a policy area. I have mentioned several ways an individual may exercise power in such an organized unit. In bureaucratic units, there is obviously the claim of legitimacy that goes with position, that is, authority, and the occupancy of a central position for dealing with a particular matter. In a bureaucratic or legislative unit, the leader can also control the conditions important to its members in such a way as to reward cooperation. And there is the important, independent effect of reputation. Some combination of these factors is generally at work whenever an individual manages to get his views generally adopted in a particular area of the unit's work or throughout its entire operation. But there is a final source of influence within an organized unit: the capability to elicit the willingness of the unit's members to follow loyally and without close calculation of risks and benefits because the individual's leadership serves their shared purposes. The subject is leadership.

The members of an organization—whether it is a bureaucratic unit or a committee or a legislative body—recognize two primary forms of group needs. The overall influence of the unit and the benefits in resources and prestige that come with influence depend upon the unit's reconciling its members' goals with the outside demands and purposes of other powerful individuals and institutions in the political environment. The unit gets power and resources by meeting others' needs. The members recognize this and know that maintaining its productive relationships with other organizations, individuals, and political bodies requires concerted action under some direction. To the extent that an individual manages this crucial responsibility effectively for them, the members of an organization will accept his or her leadership.

The unit has another set of demands: fairness and consideration in allocating the benefits and burdens of the unit's work among its members. The benefits may be influence on ultimate policy or prestige or office space or what you will. The burdens may be work or acceptance of losses. The participants realize that there will be benefits and burdens for each of them and that someone must allocate these. A just and considerate allocator becomes a leader as well.

Wilbur Mills was influential with the Ways and Means Committee, and exercised great influence in the House and in the government at large through that committee, because he served its purposes, not simply because of the resources he commanded with regard to other members. The committee as a whole sought prestige, power, and an effect on policy consistent with the views of its members but recognized that these depended upon its recommendations' remaining consistent with the electoral needs and policy views of the membership of the House. Mills's ability to satisfy environmental demands while maximizing, within this constraint, the goals of the committee membership was one of the reasons the other members of the committee followed him.

Another reason was his willingness to serve fairly the individual purposes of the members. Considering their proposals for bills and their views on other proposals was more than generosity; it built a willingness to accept his leadership that was itself a resource. Even before the radical restructuring of chairmen's powers in the early 1970s, a committee could sharply constrain the actions of its chairman, albeit with great difficulty, if it wanted to badly enough. Keeping the members from wanting to accomplish this is part of a chairman's arsenal of influence.

Even when one is dealing with a hierarchical organization and with subordinates who are expected to carry out directives from above, leadership in this final sense carries an influence that goes well beyond the limits of authority. In a bureaucratic unit, willing acceptance of leadership is loyalty, and loyalty reaches far beyond the commands of authority. I noted above that authority can be ignored unless compliance can be monitored and sanctions imposed, although any such defiance may bear the burden and vulnerability of being seen as illegitimate. But there is also a realm of legitimate discretion that is vested in subordinates. Authoritative directions, even reasonably and fairly construed, do not reach and control the multitude of decisions that the superior expects subordinates to make. Many of these decisions cannot be or are not anticipated at the time directives are issued. Yet what the leader would want, the direction he means to set for the unit, can be a source of guidance if the subordinates want it to be, if his leadership is willingly and loyally accepted. Thus the range of control that comes with eliciting willing support as a result of serving the organization's needs far exceeds what comes with authority alone.

What I have said in earlier chapters about the experience of Ann Gorsuch at the EPA and of William Olson and William Harvey at the Legal Services Corporation are reminders of the other side of this coin. In extreme cases, when the bureaucratic leader's directives are not serving the purposes of other powerful actors who can substantially affect the welfare of the unit and when those inside the organization feel it is being guided unwisely and, perhaps, that they are being treated unfairly, authority may even be openly defied, for the risks are then greatly reduced. The superiors of the individual in charge of an organization and the legislators who provide it with authority and resources generally recognize the importance of supporting the power of those with formal authority. They want someone to be accountable; they recognize that someone has to be able to give orders in the unit.

But this desire and recognition, powerful in its ability to elicit support from these outsiders for a unit's manager in his conflict with subordinates, is limited and bounded by the desire of legislators and superiors to see the unit serve something approximating their purposes. When it is clear that this desire is not being met, defiance of the manager's authority by lower levels of the organization seems far less objectionable, perhaps even something to be protected. Effective subordinates have been able to challenge successfully and indeed get rid of superiors who have not recognized that leadership requires preserving the influence of the unit with those it is expected to serve and dealing fairly with its members.

11 *Reshaping the Political Environment*

Just as legislators and government managers seek to collect advantages of personal influence (resources) to help control what will happen in certain areas of legislative or executive choice, they may also try to arrange the broader context of advantages (the setting) so as to make more likely particular policy decisions. Just as political actors must make their decisions in light of an understanding of the impact of their actions or a governmental choice on their resources of future influence, they must similarly consider the impact on the receptivity of other actors to particular policy proposals.

Beyond the Domain of Everyday Tactics

The set of likely legislative decisions available to a political actor are, in the short run, constrained by the following factors. A number of people with their own interests, beliefs, and concerns already occupy relatively powerful positions and thus can play important roles in the formal process of making the decision. Senators Hatch and Weicker occupied such positions, for example, in the battle over the Legal Services Corporation. Others with the capacity to affect the future welfare of the first set of players or to assert claims based on their responsibilities or prior acts also have relatively fixed beliefs and concerns. The American Bar Association and the Conservative Caucus fit in this category in the LSC battle. Both of these groups have distinct reputational stakes in the appearances of power and influence that come from the playing out of the political contest. Even when all this is in place, there is "play" within the setting, that is, there is room for tactics and a variety of possible outcomes. Tactics were important to the survival of the LSC. Still, much has been constrained; many possible decisions have been made extremely unlikely and some are made much more probable than others. Some are so improbable that they will never find their way on to the agenda of busy and practical decisionmakers.

But, with time and planning, some constraints can be removed, some paths smoothed; the setting shifts. The occupants of positions of authority can be changed. The powers that go with positions can be changed. The interests and beliefs of officials and private constituents can be changed. With these changes much that seemed beyond the realm of practicality becomes possible. New proposals can find their way on to the agenda.

Such changes are, of course, constantly taking place as a result of a wide variety of events whose political impact no one has planned. Office holders retire or die. The interests of powerfully placed political actors shift as industry shifts to different parts of the country. The birth control pill and an Arab oil embargo can profoundly change beliefs and concerns in such important areas of public policy as women's rights and energy. So can the failure of a war in Vietnam or against poverty, for the successes or failures of government policies are important determinants of beliefs about the future possibilities for government action.

Doubtless these unplanned events play a far greater role than any political actor's calculations in changing the boundaries of possible or plausible government action in any particular area. Still, to a lesser extent, the planned efforts of policy actors can shift the boundaries. The stage of opportunities can be reset. It is to this possibility that I now turn.

There are two broad ways to reset the stage for political action over a medium-length time horizon.

1. The first and simplest path lies in the direction of shifting those individuals whose viewpoints and objectives the political actor wants to advance into positions that enjoy unusual power and influence or increasing the power of the positions they already occupy. Thus President Reagan could redirect national policies on covert action by making William Casey CIA Director and could further the policies he shared with Vice Admiral John Poindexter by giving the National Security Council authority over sales of arms to Iran.

2. A political actor can, alternatively, address the difficult task of changing the interests and perceptions or, occasionally, even the beliefs of

powerful officials or organizational units, of organized interest groups that can bring their weight to bear on officials or committees, or of far wider publics. Such a planned change, decades ago, underpins the present reluctance of the president and Congress to attack medicare or social security benefits. How that change was brought about will provide my final example of the management of politics.

Increasing the Influence of Supporters

There are several ways of increasing the influence of those who are sympathetic to one's goals. Most obviously, one can change the occupants of positions of concentrated power, thereby bringing the influence that comes with the resources of those positions to the support of a different set of beliefs. Elections are intended to give voters the opportunity to do this with regard both to the members of Congress and to the president. After an election the president enjoys the power to appoint several thousand individuals with interests and beliefs allied to his views and thus to replace those with different inclinations. The occupants of positions of power within each house of Congress can also be changed by national elections or by party caucuses.

Without changing the occupants, one can change the resources that go with the positions, create new positions, or eliminate old ones. The creation of 120 subcommittees in the House has reduced the power of full committee chairs and of the leadership. The creation of budget committees lessened the influence of the authorizing and appropriating committees; the creation of intelligence committees did the same thing with regard to the committees formerly charged with this responsibility as part of a wider jurisdiction over foreign relations. Reallocating resources among positions alters in important ways the configuration of sympathetic or hostile resources around a particular policy. Support of health or education programs would be harder to win after budget committees, which are judged by the deficit they allow, became more powerful relative to authorizing and appropriating committees. Finally, important changes in the setting can be worked simply by changing the rules of process that determine the conditions under which items are considered.

There is no better way to examine these three possibilities than to take an extended look at three dramatic examples. Each involves a carefully planned effort to change the setting for certain more or less sharply defined types of policy. Together they illustrate the importance of legislative efforts that go well beyond seeking a particular piece of legislation—that aim instead to create the conditions for a broad set of favorable policy outcomes.

STRUCTURAL REFORM IN THE HOUSE

The structural reforms I shall describe were intended to bring about very broad changes in the types of measures that the House of Representatives was likely to accept. For the sake of concreteness, though, one typical measure can provide an example. Until 1975, the benefits of an unjustifiably generous tax deduction for depletion of oil reserves were securely in the hands of the large oil companies. I have reviewed in the last chapter the powers of those on the Ways and Means Committee, and particularly the resources of its chairman, Wilbur Mills, who defended the depletion allowance vigorously. The committee enjoyed immense advantages in the process of congressional review of tax legislation. For many years the Speaker of the House, Sam Rayburn, had made support of the depletion allowance a condition of appointment to the Ways and Means Committee. Thus a policy protective of the oil interests was all but guaranteed.

Individuals seeking to reduce the advantages enjoyed by the depletion allowance had to reduce the advantages enjoyed by its proponents. That was accomplished in the early 1970s. In the last chapter I argued that leadership involves satisfying the followers that the leader is serving their needs both in terms of a fair distribution of burdens and benefits and in terms of maintaining the resources of the organization by serving the purposes for which it was created. The committee chairmen with power under the controlling arrangements of the House before 1970 were not continuing to fulfill these functions for a changing membership in a changing environment. It was therefore possible to end their mandate. Two groups—liberal members of the Democratic majority and more impatient junior members elected in the turbulent late 1960s and early 1970s felt they were not receiving a fair distribution of benefits, particularly a fair share of influence over policy. Moreover, there was a widespread sense within the House that the committees and the body as a whole were not playing the role demanded of them by the public, and this was threatening to all members at the polls. The House seemed out of tune with the times and with voter demands.

In the early 1970s an alliance of more junior representatives, members more liberal than the chairmen controlling the House, and private organizations like Common Cause, whose power lay in access to well-organized constituent groups and the media, saw that their interests and beliefs coincided in a particular shift of structure, formal powers, and processes. Reducing the advantages of the chairmen and increasing the accessibility of House decisions to attentive voters—their common agenda—could both redistribute power *and* make the House more liberal. The necessary steps were justified by strongly held notions that representatives should be more equal in influence and more accountable to their constituents. These were accomplishable aims, because the crucial changes could be directed by the majority party in the House and a majority of the Democratic members were either junior or liberal or responsive to organizations like Common Cause or persuaded by arguments of equality and accountability at a time when the Congress was under attack.

By 1975, when the depletion allowance was eliminated for large, integrated oil companies, all the former advantages of the supporters of depletion had been changed by the purposeful activity of the reformers. Committees could no longer be "stacked" so easily by the Speaker or Chairman Mills. The caucus of the Democratic members of the House had created a new system which substantially broadened the range of policy views that were brought to bear in the process of choice of members for positions on committees. The new membership of the Ways and Means Committee was no longer homogeneous on the issue of depletion. At the same time the Democratic members of that committee had lost the great bargaining power that had come with being the body that made committee assignments and selected chairmen for other committees.

The Rules Committee could now be overruled by the Democratic Caucus in deciding what tax matters would be voted on by the full House, what amendments would be in order, and under what conditions the debate would take place. Thus to the extent that the majority of Democratic members of the House had beliefs about the depletion allowance that were substantially different from those of Ways and Means, the stage was set for different policy outcomes by amendment on the floor. At the same time the committee's bargaining advantage from having almost complete control of results in the tax area was reduced.

Similarly, the powers of Chairman Mills had been greatly reduced by the time he lost the depletion battle. Committee chairmen were now to be chosen by secret ballot every two years. Mills had to consider his new constituency of Democratic members. He had lost the absolute power to call meetings, to control staff, to decide whether there would be subcommittees and who would be on them, and to determine the jurisdiction of each subcommittee. To whatever extent the chairman's views differed from those of his committee, now broadened to include more liberal representatives, policy would be different because of the reorganization.

Public reactions could now have more sway. Depletion had always been considered an unjustified, perhaps corrupt, advantage by much of the general public; but the influence of the media, through the response of voters, depends upon access to crucial decisions and identification of the positions representatives take on an issue. The old rules had denied these prerequisites. Reforms in the early 1970s allowed recorded votes on amendments to bills, for a time opened to the public "mark-up" sessions in which a committee shaped its final recommendations, and allowed members to force a vote of all members of the majority party on any rule limiting amendments on the floor. The effect of each of these changes was to increase the power, and thus to favor the policy proposals, of groups and institutions that could effectively mobilize sizable or well-financed groups of concerned constituents.

In the decade and more that has followed these changes, adjustments and reactions have modified the anticipated effects and once again shifted power. Chairmen and committee members must still look over their shoulders at the reaction of the Democratic Caucus to their decisions. Chairman Aspin was almost deposed. But they retain more freedom and are less accountable than was once expected. A burgeoning of recorded votes led to a wide acceptance of more rules restricting amendments on the floor, and this strengthened the influence of the leadership, which shapes such rules. Members in turn have learned new ways of exercising influence on the leadership, sometimes merely by threatening to withhold support on the floor. But the fundamental point remains. Changes in process change the configuration of resources of influence and thus create predictable advantages for some policy views and dangers for others.

THE CREATION OF A CONGRESSIONAL BUDGET PROCESS

In chapter 8 I reviewed the traditional processes for authorizing and appropriating funds. I did not, however, look at these processes in a critical way. The fact of the matter is that the congressional budget process had not worked effectively for many years before the late 1970s, if one defines effectiveness as an ability to consider, at the same time, the amount the federal government will spend in a year and the amount it will receive in the form of revenues. Prior to the passage of the Congressional Budget Act in 1974, the processes that determined the amount of revenue to be raised and the amount of money to be spent by the federal government were totally unconnected. Even the process determining spending was so disaggregated as hardly to amount to a choice in any sense of the term. The continuing failures of the budget process should not obscure the real changes the Budget Act brought about.

Prior to 1974 the system worked like this. Authorizing committees in each house could recommend the approval of programs. If each house concurred and the president signed the bill, a law created the program. Programs took two major forms for budgetary purposes. Some programs distributed funds as a matter of right to particular classes of individuals or government units. No further appropriation was necessary (or, more accurately, appropriations were a mere formality) so long as the recipients satisfied the criteria specified by the program. By 1981 these "entitlements" amounted to 50 percent of the total federal budget. For the other programs, no funds could be obligated or spent by a federal agency until there had been a decision in the form of an appropriation.

Appropriations always began in the House of Representatives, where subcommittees developed recommendations on the amount of total funding (within a very high ceiling set by the statute that authorized the program). The House appropriations subcommittees prided themselves on being fiscally conservative. Their recommendations were generally adopted without substantial change by the full House Appropriations Committee and then by the House as a whole. The Senate appropriations process functioned as an appeal from the stringency of the House process. A conference, frequently splitting the difference between the two figures, would determine the amount ultimately appropriated.

The president could of course veto an entire bill but no particular part of it. Each year the Congress would pass a number of separate appropriations bills. There was no occasion where the total was pulled together or where trade-offs were forced. In this context, only the president, who proposed a budget at the start of each year, assumed a responsibility for budgetary totals, but his ability to shape the outcome of the process was severely limited. The veto of particular measures, or the threat of veto, was his only instrument until President Nixon tried unsuccessfully to impound appropriated funds.

There were a variety of consequences of this system. The president could effectively point out the irresponsibility of the Congress in budgetary matters. He was right. A set of major decisions affecting the economy of the United States was in practice beyond the reach of effective congressional power. The system as a whole did not force trade-offs between competitive claims for funds. Interest groups and others supportive of a program could concentrate their attention on a particular authorization committee and, often, an appropriations subcommittee. The membership of the committee or subcommittee was already largely self-selected because of its interest in supporting the programs within its jurisdiction. Reciprocity, deference to the expertness of the committees that had looked in most detail at a matter, and a general morality of live-and-let-live among the committee chairmen together produced an atmosphere in which each program was considered separately and sympathetically. A senior congressman could advise a new member: ''Vote for every new program and for every tax reduction; vote against any raising of the debt ceiling.''

This was a structure of advantages designed to favor the supporters of programs and expenditures and to disfavor those whose primary concern was fiscal. Seeing this bias, the supporters of a new budget process in the Congress (Senator Edmund Muskie in 1974 and then Senators Howard Baker and Pete Domenici with the coming of the Reagan administration) developed a process designed to reduce the relative advantages of the supporters of new programs. In each house a new committee was created, the Budget Committee, whose central concern was fiscal. It was charged with hearing from the other committees early in the session and then, still early, proposing an overall ceiling and some significant division of that ceiling into expenditures for different areas and programs. The proposal of the budget committees was to be voted on by each house by May 15 and then given teeth by directives to authorizing committees to report back recommended changes in their programs (or reductions in the ceilings on funding of these programs) and to the appropriations committees not to report bills exceeding a total set in the budget resolutions.

Only the process was to be changed; the same 435 representatives and 100 senators would make the ultimate decisions on the budget subject to presidential veto. But changes in process change advantages. Under the proposed change, the first issue to be addressed in a binding way was to be the overall budget and its division into major categories for various committees. On these questions the advice and recommendations to each house would come from the budget committees, the party leaders, and the president—and, significantly, would be addressed in the context of fiscal policy. On the budget issues of overall total expenditures (and various other program changes to satisfy fiscal requirements), much of the expertise justifying deference on the floor and the delegated responsibility that carries discretion with it were transferred from the authorizing and appropriating committees to a new set of hands.

The other committee chairmen could be involved, but their role would be substantially reduced. For one thing, the face of the issue would be fiscal, not programmatic. For another, the context would involve obvious competition for funding among the programmatic concerns of various committees, unlike the previous situation where each committee had to meet only a generalized argument that the budgetary impact of its decisions was excessive. Now any increase in one function or one committee's allocation would come at the direct and obvious expense of others. And constituents of a particular program would be in a far weaker position to influence those who have a crucial role in determining the amount available for that program, since that responsibility shifted from a large number of committees where constituent ties were well-established to the new budget committee.

The most successful use of the 1974 Budget Act was in the first year of President Reagan's tenure, 1981, when wholly unprecedented cuts in appropriated sums were made by adding to the May budget recommendations adopted by each house a "reconciliation" order to the legislative committees to reduce sharply the amount authorized for a number of programs over the next several years. (Since then, the Congress has retained early reconciliation orders but only for entitlement programs and revenue changes. It has dropped the application of early reconciliation to authorized spending limits, substituting the promulgation of a relatively binding ceiling on total appropriated amounts at the time of the budget recommendations early in each session. The ceiling on appropriations is then allocated by the appropriations committees among their subcommittees, and a variety of procedural devices are used, with mixed success, to prevent any casual disregard of the ceiling.)

When, in the ensuing years, even the structural changes of the 1974

Budget Act proved inadequate to give primacy to fiscal concerns over policy interests, largely because of an inability of the House, the Senate, and the president to reach agreement on where cuts should be made and whether taxes should be increased, the further structural changes of the Gramm-Rudman Act of 1985 were adopted—again in an effort to change results by changing the process. But this time a Supreme Court holding of unconstitutionality cut short the experiment in the use of process to control substance.

BLOCK GRANTS

The 1981 budget process was accompanied by a Republican and presidential push for block grants to the states of large sums of money to replace monies otherwise spent on a sizable number of discrete federal programs. The states were to exercise their own discretion in allocating sums, within such limits as the Congress chose to set. Block grants presented another dramatic example of using changes in structure and procedure to alter the advantages some policies enjoy.

Congressional decisions on block grants would importantly shape the terms of competition for favor among policies. This central fact lay behind abstract arguments based on principles of federalism. Consider one example, the area of health programs, where the Senate Labor and Human Resources Committee controlled the scope of any substitution of unrestricted block grants for defined federal benefit programs.

What were the political underpinnings of support for any health program funded by the federal government in 1981? Support depended upon: the views and sympathies of the relevant committees and the members of each house of Congress, the effectiveness of organized constituency lobbying by providers or representatives of beneficiaries, the attitudes of a national and local press, and the support of federal executive bureaus and departments. In a broader context, the level of support also depended on a history of assumptions about what the responsibilities of federal, state, and local governments for various health programs would be; on relatively established compromises among the competing demands of health and non-health programs at each level of government; and on understandings about an acceptable level of taxation at each level and about the price of greater taxation in lost votes or industry.

Shifting to the state level responsibility for deciding which health programs would be funded and in what amounts, even if there were no accompanying reduction in federal funding, would change every aspect of this complicated equation. The total amount of federal funds provided would no longer depend on established patterns of funding, the views of the executive branch, or even the views of members of Congress about particular programs and concern about their supporting constituencies. The policy concerns determining federal support for block grants would be largely the more generalized needs of states for support, and state officials would be the affected constituency. Within the total funding provided a state by the federal government, the allocation of funds to particular programs would change dramatically, for individual states would now decide in light of the radically different context of political choice at the state level.

Programs newly added to state responsibilities would have to compete with long-term claimants on state funds and also with the demands for tax reduction in this different setting. Constituency groups organized at a national level would have the tasks of reorganizing at the level of fifty separate states. There would be no executive branch support at the state level for many of the transferred programs—only for the older state programs. Conflicts between state and local officials would play major roles in state-level decisions. Traditions, assumptions, history, and networks of relationships would all change; so would the character of the decision-making body and the nature of the constituency pressures it feels.

No one could predict the detailed results of such tidal shifts. But some broad conclusions were clear. No categorical program that had been established and supported by the federal government could expect to do as well at a state level. The entire structure of political support that sustained it as a federal program would be stripped away. Its supporters would have to start fresh, building new organizational capabilities in fifty states in unequal competition with *both* older and better-connected claimants for state funds *and* restive taxpayers. The strongest supporters of replacing specific health programs with block grants to the states (President Reagan and Senator Orrin Hatch, chairman of the Senate committee) knew they would be stripping the political base from the set of programs transferred to block grants and intended just that. The most determined opponents on the committee (Senators Edward Kennedy, Robert Stafford, and Lowell Weicker) knew this too and would fight that result, supported by the interest groups threatened by the change.

Changing Interests, Perceptions, and Beliefs

INTERESTS

Without changing the occupants of positions and without changing the resources of those positions or the process through which decisions are made, fundamental changes in the setting can be accomplished by shifting the interests of those who currently enjoy advantages in the political setting. Again, the processes here are familiar.

The potential of organized or well-financed electoral support for an elected official or, alternatively, for his opponent can change the official's position on many issues, moving it in the direction of those who can choose whether to support the official or his opponent. An organized National Rifle Association has thus changed the position on gun control of even liberal members of the House of Representatives. Environmental groups that could claim the defeat of congressmen opposed to environmental initiatives in the early 1970s had their effect.

Large contributors representing oil interests undoubtedly shaped the views of members of the Senate Finance Committee in 1975. Six years later, competition for campaign contributions from independent oil producers, pitting the Reagan administration against Democratic leaders in the House, produced substantial tax advantages for independent oil in the 1981 tax-cut legislation and a year after that preserved those advantages despite the 1982 tax increase. The interest of the president and of key representatives in maintaining the favor of oil producers was as evident in the battle over President Reagan's tax initiative in 1985 in the House and a year later in the Senate as it had been a decade earlier.

As Congressman Les Aspin saw, the Defense Department can affect the position of a member of the Armed Services Committee by placing an important contract or base within his jurisdiction. In his later decisions the member will have to recognize the constituent interests created by that action. If the member's interests extend to a next job or political advancement, the case is even more dramatic. When Wilbur Mills sought the presidency, his actions on Ways and Means had to change to reflect a national electorate. It was at this time that he first supported a permanent cost-of-living adjustment in social security benefits. The same is true for any elected official who seeks an office with a wider constituency. Redistricting has the same effect.

Far more sweeping in its impact is the effect of satisfying the demands of powerful groups. Protecting and deferring to the interests of the independent oil producers, for example, removed them from an alliance with the giant integrated companies in the battle over the depletion allowance in 1975. The process is very general and extremely important. When the political force behind a policy initiative comes from a coalition of a number of groups, it is almost always possible to weaken the force of the coalition by satisfying the demands of some of the members. This possibility grandly shapes the course of policy development. It is even at work in situations where there is no organizational or interest-based division among the members of the coalition but simply differences in intensity of feeling.

A policy decision to move slowly in the direction urged by a coalition will eliminate the active participation of those who feel less intensely about the matter. Gradual withdrawal of troops from Vietnam—moving in the right direction—greatly weakened the force of the antiwar movement during the early years of the first Nixon administration. Of course, counterforces come into play in these situations. An argument for equal treatment of all those similarly situated becomes stronger when the demands of some have been satisfied. Meeting partial demands creates a precedent that can be used by others. And limited success encourages further efforts by showing the prospects of further change. But the net result of these competing forces unleashed by partially satisfying a group's demands is often to weaken the coalition, with important effects on the future prospects of policies in the area.

Other ways of changing the interests of powerful private actors and thus of officials responsive to them are important but less direct in their impact. The satisfaction of one demand of a group, such as the elderly or environmentalists, shifts the interests of their leaders to another issue if they hope to maintain the organization as a political force. If the Clean Air Act largely satisfies one set of demands of environmentalists, perhaps toxic waste disposal will become a more pressing priority. The enactment of one measure can create new concerns and needs for important private or government actors, thereby changing the prospects of other measures. The passage of early programs of medical assistance for the poor resulted in substantial new costs for state and local governments. The predictable political result was that the substantial political influence of mayors and governors was available to those who later proposed programs that involved federal assumption of these costs. When the Federal Communications Commission decided to require television stations to provide free time for antismoking commercials to counteract commercials for cigarette manufacturers, networks became willing to accept a total ban on televised ads for cigarettes. In 1987 pharmaceutical manufacturers fought federal payments for drugs in cases of catastrophic illness, anticipating that a demand for federal price controls would soon follow.

Changing the way in which interests are perceived by political actors can be as important as changing their interests. Once a benefit becomes an expectation, groups begin to rely on it. Expectations built into the fabric of everyday life are defended with a strength that is not available to those seeking new advantages. Eliminating farm benefits is a far more difficult task than failing to grant them in the first place. Interests justified by more general arguments of equity or long tradition involve double stakes. It is not only the benefits that are at issue; it is also the position of the group in society and its ability to defend that position.

ATTITUDES, CONCEPTS, AND BELIEFS

The Stability of Presumptions about the Proper Roles of Government. Most political actors react to the merits of an initiative primarily in terms of their views as to whether there should be more government activity in the area and, if the proposal moves government in the desired direction, secondarily in terms of a crude judgment as to whether the proposed program will be a moderately intelligent effort. Whether the program's benefits exceed its costs by some technical or "objective" system of measurement is generally unimportant to an actor who has long wanted more governmental attention to area X, the area this proposal "at last" addresses. For him the alternative, rejecting the proposal, means that the attention (and resources) may be given to areas where the political actor sees fewer benefits. Moreover, he generally gives great weight to the costs of inaction in the area of his concern. Finally, he hardly has the time or information necessary to make technical judgments about optimal programs. Arriving at broad judgments about the desirability of government activity in each of a half-dozen or dozen areas is a big enough job. The judgment may take the cautious form of a set of presumptions subject to change if a strong enough case is made in a particular instance. But the presumption will control most matters.

Some of the ingredients of these crucial judgments are very hard to change. They relate in complicated ways to personal, group, and constituent interests not only in what is done but also in what is conveyed to the public by the symbolism of whatever is decided; to matters of status created by roles in government actions; to personality and experiences from childhood; and to the very language, concepts, and myths in which we have come to conceptualize social problems and government responses.

One may be deeply suspicious of government regulation (or, alternatively, of an unregulated market in some commodity or service) for reasons too fundamental to be changeable by argument. The same is true of assessments of the dangers of Russian expansionism (or of the domestic military-industrial complex); of the harmful effects on individual responsibility of welfare (or of the dangers of public callousness to the helplessness of the poor); and of the risks of crime (as opposed to those of increased police powers).

Such beliefs may not change fundamentally without some massive stimulus—an unsuccessful war, a depression, widespread social unrest, the apparent failure of an immense government effort in an area, or an event as important to foreign policy as the split between the U.S.S.R. and China. At least there may be no basic change in the absence of a sweeping shift in public or constituent attitudes brought about by some such events, perhaps as interpreted by a newly elected president. Stage setting in terms of beliefs and attitudes must work within these constraints.

Responsibility to Consider the Evidence. Cutting across relatively firmly held beliefs about the proper role of government in a particular area are pragmatic notions of the obligation to learn from experience and to defer to common sense. Voters, legislators, and elected executives all learn from the success or failure of prior program initiatives. If it becomes established wisdom that the Great Society programs did not work, similar programs are unlikely to be undertaken for some time. The clearest modern examples are provided by the war in Vietnam. The various "lessons" of that traumatic experience will shape our foreign policy for decades. On the other hand, because the "safety net" of social security has worked, it will be exceedingly difficult to try to "fix" that program.

In areas where there has been no prior government activity, debate about the wisdom of government involvement is likely to turn on whether there is really a problem appropriate for government action. That depends on two matters of relatively unshakable faith and one of evidence. As to faith, the issues are whether private arrangements and the market will handle the problem and whether the burdens and inefficiencies of government involvement are likely to outweigh whatever success is predictable from prior government activities in other areas. But such broad convictions about what roles the market and government can and should play in a particular area are almost always presumptions, rebuttable in specific circumstances by sufficiently clear evidence of need.

Thus the first auto safety legislation succeeded, in large part, because Ralph Nader could point to evidence that the market had in fact failed. Millions of autos had been determined to be unsafe by the automobile manufacturers themselves and yet they had not taken corrective steps. Conversely, it was the *absence* of evidence as to how many drivers would leave operational the passive restraints in their cars that allowed the NHTSA administrator Raymond Peck to operate on a presumption against more regulation (which meant, in his case, that the government should not require passive restraints in every car). In an analogous way, evidence that the oil companies were reaping immense tax-free profits after the Arab oil embargo of 1973 eliminated the long-accepted justification for the special tax treatment of oil depletion—a belief that tax benefits were a necessary supplement to market incentives to drill.

At a slightly earlier stage, the decision to gather evidence or have the federal government develop the facts is important in the same way. A decision to collect data on the health needs of the elderly set the stage for later arguments about medicare. A decision to undertake a study of the consequences of certain safety devices in automobiles affected the later debate about whether they should be required. When Secretary William Coleman announced in 1976 that 12,000 lives could be saved each year by airbags or other passive restraints, the contest for policy allegiance was shaped both by the available factual information and the stark definition of the choice in two measured terms, lives and money.

Information must be reduced to manageable, lucid form if it is to have an impact on officials or legislatures or the public. Evidence must be understandable and simple. Debates about obligations to the poor and the responsiveness of government have been shaped for decades by the development of an accepted, durable definition of poverty in terms of family size and income adjusted automatically for inflation. Before that there was no accepted measure of either the size of the problem or the effects of government responses. Without such measures presumptions favoring or opposing government assistance to the poor could less easily be overcome.

Recognizing all this, Budget Director David Stockman fought unsuccessfully to change the accepted definition to include as income benefits received from government programs.

Changing Beliefs by Characterizing a Situation in a New Way. What I have described so far is the effect of evidence on long-established, deeply rooted convictions as to the desirability of government activity in a particular area. There is another way of changing widespread beliefs. It involves placing a situation in a category that seems to demand (or resist) some particular form of government activity, rather than allowing the situation to be categorized in a way that has the opposite consequences for many political actors or observers.

In the background of many, if not all, decisions about the proper role of government lie a number of very widely shared beliefs about how things work and what are desirable or proper responses. Consider a few examples. A belief that "we shouldn't be pushed around as a nation" perhaps because "an aggressor who is allowed to succeed will be encouraged in his demands" may underlie many foreign policy decisions. And domestic policy is shaped by other pieces of popular wisdom. "Left to their own devices government officials will regulate more and spend more." "Misbehavior results from a lack of parental or societal discipline." "One who doesn't work doesn't deserve what others who do work get." Surely there are a hundred or more such "major premises" affecting our politics. Considerable political power is unleashed whenever a new or ambiguous event is persuasively characterized in terms these premises make relevant.

Much of the activity of political figures involves placing a situation within the familiar framework of such homilies and descriptions of the way the world works. The MX missile is described by President Reagan's supporters as "a peacekeeper." What is "star wars" to opponents of the program is a strategic *defense* initiative to others. The Contras fighting the socialist government of Nicaragua are freedom fighters. Guerrillas in El Salvador are terrorists. The term "welfare cheaters" will elicit a familiar set of reactions. A fifteen-year-old thief is a juvenile to liberals, a mugger to conservatives; and the different characterizations bring with them very different policy prescriptions.

Sometimes the connection between a familiar situation and one of the hundred or so common understandings about how social/political relations work has been made in childhood. One's parents' reactions to Franklin oosevelt's WPA may have much to do with one's view of the Legal ervices Corporation fifty years later. Sometimes major political figures, articularly presidents, have the power to persuade many people to adopt a lear characterization, within the framework of familiar major premises, f a situation that is otherwise very ambiguous. Sometimes politically ngenious appointed officials can make or shift a characterization in crucial vays. Private individuals and academics also have a role in this process of ttributing familiar meanings to ambiguous or unfamiliar events, institu- ions, or people.

Consider just a few examples. The use of the insurance concept, accom- panied by a payroll deduction, for social security retirement benefits hanged the framework in which political actors would think about old age penefits and medicare as well. People in the United States react differently o "insurance" than they do to "welfare." One represents self-reliance; he other, prolonged dependency. When Ralph Nader called attention to he importance for driver and passengers of the "container" built by the arge automobile manufacturers in allowing, causing, or preventing harm rom automobile accidents, the problem was redefined by substituting the ature of the container as a new center of policy interest and its makers as a competing locus of responsibility along with the driver. It also, of course, pecame possible to call for government agencies to develop evidence on he difference various safety devices could make.

The depletion allowance was, by 1974, no longer accepted as a reflec- ion of the cost of doing business; it was seen as an incentive to exploration. It could be recognized by then in terms of a new concept, as a "tax expenditure." This was no accident. Six years before, when Stanley Sur- rey was concluding his tenure as assistant secretary of the treasury for tax policy, he began to develop, and in the ensuing years to propagate, a new conception of those tax deductions and credits that were not merely the costs of doing business, that is, that were not simply devices for arriving at *net* income. He brought first the Treasury Department, then the congres- sional taxing committees, and finally the budget committees to define such tax benefits as "tax expenditures," comparable in most respects to any budgeted and appropriated expenditures.

Conceiving these deductions and credits as a cost incurred by the gov- ernment for its purposes, rather than as an inseparable part of the compli- cated process for determining how much each person owes in taxes, radi- cally changes the definition of the situation for policymakers. Those who oppose government expenditures *and* taxation may now see any deduction that is not justifiable as a step in measuring net income as an undesirable government expense for a program (rather than as a reduction in burdensome taxation). Those who want to assess who gets what from the government now often include "tax expenditures" as well as welfare. David Stockman has described President Reagan's adamant hostility to the concept of tax expenditures. The president recognized its political potency.

What is important to see is not only the range but the power of the phenomena of characterizing new events or even old situations in terms that plug directly into powerful views of wide publics as to how the world works and what behavior is desirable. When in the spring of 1986 an American was killed and many more injured by a terrorist bomb explosion in Berlin, the Reagan administration had to, and did, concern itself with how and when information connecting the bombing to Libyan support would be revealed. As soon as a tight connection was made, millions of Americans would relate the event to a whole set of powerfully motivating, closely related, long-held beliefs and attitudes. Everything from experiences with childhood bullies to a proudly learned history of American responses to aggression would almost automatically create a powerful political demand as soon as the bombing was seen as a planned, purposeful act of a foreign government already characterized as extremely hostile. President Carter paid a great price for apparent helplessness in dealing with bullying, insulting outrages by Iranian crowds when they held American hostages. President Reagan paid a great price for secretly selling arms to Iran's leaders.

One particularly powerful major premise shaping the views of most Americans is the concept of fairness, both in the sense of similar treatment of people similarly situated and in the sense of honoring expectations. A departure from fairness in either sense threatens the trust in equal societal membership of those who feel that their claims to fall under the major premise are relatively clear. For these reasons, it makes a great difference politically whether matters important to any group are categorized as merely "interests" or "the demands of parity or equal treatment" or "legitimate expectations" or, most compellingly, "rights."

Thus, it was almost as important to the history of social security that the language of debate changed from an "interest" in retirement benefits for the elderly to a "right" as it was that a perception of this shared interest developed in a group with substantial political power. The willingness of

olitical actors to pursue their interests depends, in short, upon their sense
f the legitimacy of the interest and the unfairness of denying it recogni-
ion. Changing either of these factors also changes the setting for particular
olicy proposals.

*Bringing about Changes in the Broadest Notions about the Proper Roles of
Government.* We have looked at the stability of presumptions about the
oles of government in general and in particular areas and at the type of
evidence or, alternatively, recharacterization that may overcome those
presumptions in particular, limited areas of government activity. There is a
ast dramatic possibility, however. Sometimes large numbers of people
will modify their broadest notions of the role of government in the face of
he apparent failure of an entire prior philosophy. The coming of the New
Deal in the wake of the Great Depression was such a time. So, perhaps, has
been the conservative tide of the late 1970s and the Reagan presidency,
although the polling evidence and election returns are far from clear on this
point.

There can rarely be convincing evidence of the failure of a view so broad
as that the federal government should (or should not) be active in regulat-
ing the domestic economy and redistributing its proceeds. Therefore, the
path of changed opinion on such matters is generally not from particular
government actions to their consequences (success or failure) and thence to
new attitudes. or even from specific evidence to a conclusion that a problem exists and a governmental solution is needed. The path of change goes,
rather, from widespread public concern about a very large problem, such
as the state of the economy (or, in another area, our national power or
prestige), through a plausible diagnosis of the source of the problem in
terms of the overall roles government and the market have been playing in
the society, and from there to changed attitudes about the role of government. Given a national tradition of preoccupation with the dangers and
potential of government, a prolonged recession (or, analogously, an unpopular foreign policy) invites explanation (and solution) in terms of the
roles properly played by government. If the explanation and solution are
first supported by experts, then adopted by opinion leaders, and finally
become part of accepted popular wisdom, a new and politically powerful
set of beliefs about the role of government will be in place.

The conservative tide beginning in the late 1970s was fueled by a
faltering economy for which government actions or omissions may have

had little responsibility. Yet a widespread belief, at least in Congress, that reducing regulation and public spending were appropriate and even necessary responses—a set of policies recommended by conservative Republicans since 1965 without enthusiastic public reaction—depended only on the apparent inefficiency and failure of many bold government initiatives, the popular dissemination of respectable academic support for these new policies, the discrediting by economic failures of the advice of the competing academics, and a trust in a pragmatic public willingness to try new things when old policies are not working.

After the 1980 election an economy that was continuing to lag badly and was plagued by inflation, together with a developing fear that economic progress might be coming to an end after a long period of sustained growth, provided all the background that was necessary for a widespread willingness to try something dramatically new—the Reagan tax and budget initiatives. Even legislators otherwise committed to the welfare state had to recognize the demand of the times for a dramatic experiment.

A Final Example

Let me end, as I began, with the appointed government manager. The focus of the first seven chapters of this book on dangers, obligations, powers that must be satisfied, and constraints might leave a picture of the role of the government manager as one who exercises choice among discrete alternatives that are defined by outside forces in the political environment. But that picture ignores the role of the manager in reshaping the political environment and thus defining his own boundaries.

Even in the short run, the job of the manager is not merely to accept constraints but to provide leadership in shaping the content of the constraints by integrating the demands of political powers and bringing out of these demands, as well as out of broader public understandings and political philosophies, an intelligible definition of activity in his area and a defensible meaning or justification of it. What is, from the point of view of the organization, a strategy is for others an intelligible set of policies and a new vision of the purpose and legitimacy of governmental action in a particular area. And new visions alter political constraints.

In the longer run, the government actor can occasionally reshape the very context of interests, attitudes, concepts, and beliefs that create his political environment. No case is more remarkable in this respect than the history of medicare and the leading role of Wilbur Cohen, who worked in this area as a government manager for decades before becoming secretary of the Department of Health, Education and Welfare in the late 1960s. Emphasizing any very dramatic example may mislead as to more common prospects. But such examples also clarify the most powerful and lasting possibilities of political management.

Government-sponsored health insurance had been considered in the United States as early as 1912, when Theodore Roosevelt made it a central feature of an aggressive party platform. The Franklin Roosevelt administration almost included it in the social security package of 1935. Senator Robert Wagner introduced it in Congress in 1939 and 1941. After Truman's election in 1948, the new president proposed national health insurance. As a result of ideological opposition on the ground of alleged socialism and a massive lobbying campaign (one that cost about one and a half million dollars even in those early days) conducted by the American Medical Association (AMA), the proposal was soundly defeated. Many of its congressional supporters lost their seats in the next election.

Thus the situation midway in the twentieth century was hardly promising for Cohen and his associates, who had been working on government health insurance for more than a decade. Even though the notion of government assistance in meeting health needs was supported by a substantial majority of citizens, it lacked what it takes to move from a nice idea to an enacted program. It had no strongly motivated constituency. It was subject to plausible arguments that it could not be administered either effectively or without interfering with valued personal relationships between doctors and patients. The idea ran counter to a strongly conservative trend of the times. It was not supported by those who occupied strategic positions in the legislative machinery for considering such proposals and had the political resources to block or push initiatives. Chairman Walter George of the Senate Finance Committee, for example, was firmly opposed.

Finally, the AMA, which opposed it, was a very powerful, well-organized constituency group. Doctors were spread throughout the country and regularly met many people who were likely to be responsive to the medical profession's view on matters of health. Doctors contributed money that important legislators (or their opponents) needed in election campaigns. The AMA bought advertisements of its own. Like the business interests that coalesced against government regulatory initiatives two decades later, the AMA was able to form coalitions with other interest groups. Like the

American Bar Association in 1981, the AMA and its members were professionals of considerable status and enjoyed personal relationships with strategically placed legislators. Furthermore, they had mounted successful electoral campaigns against specific legislative supporters of national health insurance. No comparable constituency group supported national health insurance.

Supporters of national health insurance needed first to develop a comparable highly motivated and well-organized constituency. Immediately after defeat of national health insurance in 1949 and 1950, Cohen and his associates shifted to a proposal for government health insurance only for the aged, a group that was becoming a much larger percentage of the population and that voted in disproportionately heavy numbers. (By the time medicare was enacted in 1965, 22 percent of the voting population would be over 65 and strongly motivated by this issue.) The cost of universal national health insurance would clearly have to be shared by all its beneficiaries. The cost of insurance for the aged would be borne by those still working, while the substantial benefits would accrue only to those over 65. For that constituency medicare was an extremely attractive proposition.

Moreover, although there are ordinarily grave political disadvantages in imposing costs on those who will not enjoy benefits, even here there were compensations. We will all be old and enjoy the benefits at some stage. The children of those over 65, who would otherwise share the costs of medical assistance for their parents, would also benefit and could see their stake in the result. Moreover, the private business interests that might be adversely affected—companies selling medical insurance—were not interested in covering those over 65. The claims were too large. In due course, the AFL-CIO undertook to organize the constituencies that would fight for medicare. Elected officials began to see the issue as an electoral opportunity or threat.

Arguments that might persuade those not otherwise strongly committed one way or the other also had to be developed. Cohen and his associates were central here too. Could not the private market solve the problem? Presidential commissions of prestigious authorities were formed to report on facts painstakingly gathered, often by the Social Security Administration where Cohen and his associates worked. Those reports created a powerful picture of the extreme medical needs and the hopeless poverty of those over 65. Could the federal government handle such a massive federal program efficiently? That question could be answered in terms of experience; the handling of the retirement benefits of social security was obviously satisfactory, indeed highly efficient. Would not government health insurance inevitably disrupt the personal relationship between doctor and patient or compromise the doctor's independence of judgment? Cohen and his associates pressed successfully for the enactment of disability insurance during the mid-1950s; this program permitted them to provide specific evidence that government regulation of medical practice was not an inevitable consequence of government funding of a medical procedure—in that case an examination to determine disability. In the same vein, the fears of the AMA could be lessened by limiting the newer proposal to hospital costs and perhaps only a few additional medical services.

Other changes in the structure of belief surrounding government health insurance were required. The proposal would be attacked, Cohen could see, as a form of socialism or, less dramatically, as a denial of the ethic of individual responsibility for one's own needs and future. Indeed, as a matter of social philosophy, many medicare supporters might have preferred a more generous scheme of payments limited to the poor, rather than a less generous scheme available to the better off as well. But as the designers of a national political program, they saw the importance of conforming to an ideology of self-reliance—a lesson they had learned as early as 1935 in dealing with social security.

Medical insurance for the aged could be made to nestle comfortably beside social security's retirement and disability benefits and unemployment compensation. These programs were perceived as wholly consistent with the American ethic of self-reliance. The common thread is that each one provides government assistance at the very moment when even the most self-reliant cannot care for himself. The concept of insurance has been a powerful symbol of this. Insurance is, after all, what a self-reliant person buys to provide for such events. So Cohen and the other managers of the government programs dealing with social security sold "insurance," but it was called medicare.

This was not an orderly set of steps, moving inexorably forward. Pieces were put in place and held there until other necessary pieces were also present. The program had been designed to create a powerful potential constituency. In due course, the AFL-CIO undertook to organize those who would come to fight for medicare. Ambitious elected officials seek out such concerned constituencies. Senator John F. Kennedy of Massachusetts and others did. Arguments and information and evidence were developed to persuade the weakly motivated. Powerfully placed legislators who were hostile to the proposal might block action for awhile. Representative Wilbur Mills did until 1965. But the item would remain on the national agenda as long as the aged were poor, in need of medical care, politically active, and familiar with the benefits of social security. Cohen and his associates were in a position to explain the proposal to, and repeatedly press it upon, powerful legislators and presidents as the recognized experts in the operation of compulsory national insurance schemes. In 1965, President Lyndon Johnson made medicare his first priority, and Wilbur Mills led it to enactment.

Finally, Cohen and his associates knew that, once enacted, the health benefits provided would be considered a "right," indeed a right purchased as insurance. This entitlement would be defended by the elderly at the polls. Indeed, every worker paying social security taxes would have a stake in maintaining medicare for his own old age. In sum, Cohen and his associates had changed the political setting permanently, making difficult any effort to reduce or rescind the program. Medicare would survive, substantially intact, even the conservative tide of the 1980s.

If the government manager is not merely the implementer of the decisions of elected officials but, more often, the helmsman of a comparatively independent organization, guided by a strategy relating it to other such organizations as well as to elected officials; if indeed the manager can sometimes even shape the very conditions of political acceptance that bound his independence, how are we to ensure that the governors are responsible to the governed? I think the problem is more apparent than real. Consider more carefully this dramatic final example, the history of medicare, for the prominence of Wilbur Cohen's role is entirely consistent with a deep and persistent responsiveness to the forces we associate with popular control of government.

Looked at from the point of view of the manager, Cohen's task was to shape a proposal, get it on the political agenda and keep it there, develop supporting information, encourage favorable constituencies, and show that it could be implemented effectively and efficiently. He also had to make sure that the design would take root in the American political soil so that it would not easily be dislodged by shifting political winds. It is, of course, there decades later. Few managers could have hoped to accomplish this on such a scale; for, besides talent, finding a time when all the necessary pieces were in place simultaneously was only possible for Cohen and his associates because they were around for decades. Most appointed officials are around for months. Still, Cohen's accomplishment may seem far too clever and complicated to be truly democratic. Yet such a judgment would be profoundly mistaken.

Consider the same events in terms of the familiar devices of popular control. To succeed, Cohen had to find a time when the proposal, carefully designed to be consistent with powerful strands of American ideology (the work and responsibility ethics), would be seen as desirable and effective by a significant number of those attentive to the issue. There had to be at the same time a sufficient commitment from a significant organized constituency (the elderly) to offset a powerful and well-financed organized opposition (the AMA)—"sufficient" in light of the attitudes and interests of those elected officials strategically placed with the resources to advance or stall the ultimate legislative decision. Even then, success had to await an electoral mandate and a change in the occupancy of positions of national power that came with the end of the Eisenhower administration and its replacement by Kennedy and Johnson. A change in public attitudes toward the role of government and its responsibility for assuring equality and a decent level of well-being for even the most deprived had to precede or at least accompany the passage of medicare.

The manager who is prepared to seek new directions for her organization and new meanings for government activity in the area of concern, who envisages her task as creating form out of, rather than simply accepting and negotiating with, the powers and constraints surrounding her and her organization, is inevitably the agent of democratic forces. Forbidden to appeal directly to voters by federal law, she can do no more than offer that opportunity to elected officials, showing them what constituencies may want and what broader publics may come to believe. The manager can bring energy and insight to a political process that is stagnant or confused. But in doing so, the manager is no more, at best, than a partner of elected powers and a servant of those who choose them.

In the end, legitimacy belongs entirely to elected officials; farsighted yet realistic vision, often to those charged with managing the ongoing activities of government. Bringing these attributes together, the fond hope of representative democracy, is the responsibility of both.

Appendix: Kennedy School Case Studies

In writing this book, I have used detailed accounts of a number of events taken from case studies done by the John F. Kennedy School of Government. The primary references and the names of their writers follow.

1. Bureau of Security & Consular Affairs. Jeanne Johns.
2. The Case of the Segregated Schools. Eric Stern.
3. Congressman Aspin and Defense Budget Cuts. James Dillon.
4. The Depletion Allowance. Mark Kleiman.
5. Disability Insurance, Medicare and Medicaid. Dennis Aftergut.
6. A Failing Agency: The Federal Trade Commission. Randy Bellows.
7. Fraud, Abuse and Waste at HEW. David Whitman.
8. Legal Services Corporation. David Kennedy.
9. Legislating the New Federalism: Congressional Budget Process and Block Grants for Health Programs. Paul Starobin.
10. Les Aspin and the MX. David Kennedy.
11. Mike Pertschuk and the FTC. Arthur Applbaum.
12. Oversight of the Criminal Division. Nancy Dolberg.
13. The Rescission of the Passive Restraints Standard. David Kennedy.
14. Ruckelshaus and Acid Rain. Donald Lippincott.
15. Ruckelshaus Returns. Donald Lippincott.
16. Section 103 of the Internal Revenue Code. Ronald Beaulieu.

Index

ABSCAM investigation, 100–05
AFL-CIO, 186, 187
access as resource, 150–51
Adams, Brock, 84, 86
Adams regulation, 88, 89
advantages in legislative process, 112–13.
    See also resources of influence; tactics,
    legislative
agencies, government. *See* federal agen-
    cies; managers of federal agencies *and*
    individual issues and organizations
agendas, 135, 149, 158
Aid to Families with Dependent Children
    (AFDC), 49, 59
alliances, 14, 35–36, 42, 56, 75; recruit-
    ment of, 91, 130; examples of, 103–
    04, 139, 140–41; in legislative tactics,
    125, 126; taking advantage of, 134,
    136
Allison, Graham, xiv
American Bar Association (ABA), 17,
    186; FTC and, 16, 21, 22; LSC and,
    76, 77, 79, 120, 134, 164
American Medical Association (AMA),
    185–86, 187
Andrews, Kenneth, xiii
antitrust laws, 58, 59
appearances and reality, 11, 47, 48, 139;
    examples of, 49–53. *See also* Health,
    Education and Welfare, Department of
    (HEW); press

appointments, presidential, 6, 28, 57, 77.
    See also managers of federal agencies
appropriations. *See* authorization and ap-
    propriation of funds
Aspin, Les, 118, 175; on defense spend-
    ing, 137, 139–41, 142–44; MX missile
    and, 145, 146–48, 151, 152
attorney general, 57, 62–63, 64
audits, 51, 52, 54, 55
authority as source of influence, 13, 14,
    37, 38, 148–49
authorization and appropriation of funds,
    110, 111, 130; rules governing, 113–
    19; budget process, 169–73. *See also*
    block grants; Legal Services Corpora-
    tion (LSC); MX missile fight

Baker, Howard, 171
bargaining as resource, 115, 136, 152–53
beliefs, power of, 28, 125, 178, 180–83
Bell, Griffin, 56, 63, 64, 65, 66, 68, 81–
    82
block grants, 173–74
Broyhill, Jim, 32
Budget Act of *1974*, 117, 170, 172
business community, 29–32
Business Roundtable, 30
Butler, M. Caldwell, 134

Califano, Joseph, 49–53, 80
Cannon, Howard, 30

Carter, Jimmy, 27, 29, 46, 52, 54, 55, 66, 67–68, 84, 119, 146, 182
Carter administration, 30, 56, 57–58, 59, 94
Casey, William, 165
Central Intelligence Agency (CIA), 58
centrality, 153–55, 157
change in federal agencies, 5, 6–8; changing times, 10–11, 29–32; in strategies, 39–41; influence and, 165–66, 167; changing interests, 175–77
Civil Aeronautics Board, 31
civil rights issues, 57, 58, 59, 95, 102
civil servants, 13, 14
Civiletti, Benjamin, 56, 66, 68, 82
Clark, Dick, 30
Clayton Act, 16
Clean Air Act, 176
Cohen, Wilbur, 185, 186–87, 188–89
Coleman, William, 84, 179
Collier, Calvin, 26
committees, congressional, 13, 129–30, 135, 142, 143, 151, 166; power of, 30, 31, 118
Common Cause, 168
common responsibility among agencies: strategy structure, 90–91; shared organizational traits, 92–95; differences and jealousies, 96–97; "who" dimension, 97–100, 104–05. *See also* ABSCAM investigation
competition among federal agencies, 92, 99, 100, 103–04
Concept of Corporate Strategy, The (Andrews), xiii
conferences, power of, 115, 117–18
congruence, 20, 21–22
Conservative Caucus, 120, 121, 123, 132, 164
constituencies, 13, 14, 21, 80; power of, 27–29, 38, 49, 54, 63–64; private, 36, 125, 130–31, 168; taking advantage of, 134, 135–36
consumer movement, 16–17, 18, 21, 23, 26, 29–30, 32
Consumer Protection Agency, 30
Consumer Reports, 16
continuing resolution, 116–17, 120, 122, 124. *See also* Legal Services Corporation (LSC)

courts, 8, 64, 149. *See also* Supreme Court
Cox, Archibald, 9, 28
credibility, 119, 151
Curran, Gary, 77, 78

Defense Department, 46, 48, 52, 100, 101, 139, 142
defense spending: designing tactics concerning, 137–41
delay as tactic, 137
Democratic Caucus, 168, 169
Denton, Jeremiah, 120, 121, 122, 124
deregulation, 31
design, legislative, 129, 132. *See also* tactics, legislative
Dingell, John, 44
Dole, Elizabeth, 88
Domenici, Pete, 117–18, 119, 171
Downs, Anthony, xiv
Drug Enforcement Administration, 96, 99
Dunn, David, 30

Edelman, Murray, xiv
Egger, Roscoe, 69, 72
Eisenhower administration, 189
electoral issues, 5, 6, 9, 129
ends and means, 42–45
Engman, Lewis, 26
entitlements, 170
Environmental Protection Agency (EPA), 7, 8–10, 109
Errichetti, Angelo, 101
Essence of Decision (Allison), xiv
Evins, Joe, 16, 17, 20, 23
external support, 15, 19, 45, 75; changing conditions of, 40, 41; requirements for maintaining, 91–92; importance of, 98–99. *See also* constituencies; public opinion

federal agencies, 3, 6–7, 12–15; choice of activities, 11, 32–34, 38, 60, 61, 91, 92, 112; dissent within, 34–35. *See also* common responsibility among agencies; managers of federal agencies
Federal Bureau of Investigation (FBI), x, 58, 96, 99–100
Federal Communications Commission (FCC), 177

Federal Trade Commission (FTC), 15–
16, 42, 49; strategy for, 17–21, 36–40;
new goals for, 21–24; changes in, 25–
27; objectives and constituencies, 27–
28; changing times and, 29–32; decision-making in, 32–35
Federal Trade Commission Improvements
Act, 32
Fenno, Richard, xiv
filibuster, 116, 117
Ford, Gerald, 101, 102
Ford administration, 52, 84, 94
friendship in legislative tactics, 28, 111,
125, 127–28
Froman, Lewis, xiv

George, Walter, 185
Giuliani, Rudolph W., 102
goals for federal agencies, 10, 11, 12, 13,
38, 41; establishment of, 14–15; desirability and possibility, 19–21, 60; implementation of, 21–24; decisions
defining, 42, 57–58; in large agency,
59–62; presidential goals, 66–70
Gorsuch, Anne, 28, 81, 109; in EPA, 7–
11, 43–44
government, role of, 177–78; degree of
involvement of, 178–79; changing notions of, 183–84
Gramm-Rudman Act of *1985,* 173

Haig, Alexander, 80
Halperin, Morton, xiv
Hart, Phil, 30
Harvey, William, 76, 77, 78, 79–80
Hatch, Orrin, 120, 121, 122, 124, 164,
174
Health and Human Services, Department
of (HHS), 47, 59, 62
Health, Education and Welfare, Depart-
ment of (HEW), 46, 49–53, 62, 185
Hebert, F. Edward, 142–43
Heclo, Hugh, xiv
Hickel, Walter, 80
history, importance of, xi, 6, 46
Hoover, J. Edgar, xi
House Appropriations Subcommittee, 16
House Armed Services Committee, 118,
137, 138–39, 143, 153
House Judiciary Committee, 120

House Ways and Means Committee, 113,
132, 156–57, 168
Hyde, Henry J., 134

ideology, 132, 187, 189
impoundment of funds, 31, 117, 171
incompetence, 42, 43, 45, 46, 50
independence, departmental, 64–65, 66–
67, 68
influence. *See* resources of influence
inspectors general, 109–10
interest groups, 7, 8, 20, 43, 139, 140–
41, 174. *See also* constituencies; external support
Internal Revenue Service (IRS), 46, 69,
72; claiming legitimacy, 75–76
internal security, xi
investigative agencies, 96–97
investigators, federal, 95, 96, 103

Jackson, Andrew, 45
Johnson, Lyndon, 29, 119, 188, 189
Judiciary Committees, 61
Justice Department, 16, 44, 95, 101, 121;
under changing administration, 56–59;
Civil Rights Division of, 57, 59; strat-
egy in, 62–66; president and, 67–70

Kennedy, Edward, 31, 174
Kennedy, John F., ix, 148, 187–88, 189
"kid-vid," 33, 37, 38–39, 41
Kingdon, John, xiv
Kirkpatrick, Miles, 17, 26
Knight, Frances, ix, x–xi

Lavelle, Rita, 44
law, 8, 62, 72
law enforcement: agencies involved in,
93–96
leadership, 34, 38, 41, 160–63. *See also*
managers of federal agencies
"leaking" information, 48, 150
Legal Counsel, Office of, 63
Legal Services Corporation (LSC), 28,
114, 119–20; claiming legitimacy, 76–
80; strategy for re-funding, 121–24;
tactics in reauthorization, 132–34
legitimacy, 11, 38–39, 74; role of managers, 6–8, 80–83; claiming legitimacy,
75–79; in law enforcement agencies,

legitimacy (*continued*)
99, 100. *See also* Internal Revenue Service (IRS); Legal Services Corporation (LSC); National Highway Traffic Safety Administration (NHTSA)
Lewis, Drew, 84, 88
lobbying, 30, 33, 84, 121, 131, 134, 185; business lobbies, 31–32; for defense spending, 139, 140, 148
Lott, Trent, 68, 69
loyalty, 37, 41, 65, 80, 111, 155–56; to president, 71, 78–79, 80–81; among agencies, 92–93, 99; in legislative tactics, 125, 126, 127–28

Maass, Arthur, xiv
Magnuson, Warren, 17, 30
Magnuson-Moss Act (*1975*), 26, 32, 33
Management and Budget, Office of, 8, 84, 110
managers of federal agencies, 4–5, 93; setting new directions, 6–8; responsibilities, 8–10, 14–15; questions to consider, 10–12, 28–29; relation to president, 45–46, 65–66; managing appearances, 53–55; role of, 184–85, 188–89
mandates, 148–49
Mayhew, David, xiv
media: importance of, 7, 13, 14, 81, 132, 139, 168, 169
mediator, role of, 75, 80–81
medicare. *See* national health insurance
Meese, Edwin, 56, 58, 59, 61, 65, 76
Mezines, Basil, 25
Mills, Wilbur, 156, 158, 159, 161, 167, 168, 169, 188
minorities, 57–58, 59
Moral Majority, 58, 62
Morgenthau, Robert, 102
Morris, Tom, 51–52, 54
Moss, John, 30
Muskie, Edmund, 85, 171
MX missile fight, 146–48

Nader, Ralph, 15, 16, 21, 23, 31, 36, 84, 179
national health insurance, 185–88
National Highway Traffic Safety Administration (NHTSA), 83–89, 109, 179

National Rifle Association (NRA), 131, 132, 175
National Security Council (NSC), 100
Neustadt, Richard, xiv
New Right, 76, 77, 78
Nixon, Richard, 9, 17, 28, 45, 46, 117, 137, 149; FTC and, 18, 21; LSC and, 119–20
nonpolitical experts, 75, 83
North, Oliver, 148

oil depletion allowance, 167–69, 175, 176, 179, 181
Olson, William, 76, 77, 78, 79–80
Organized Crime Strike Force, 97, 101, 102–3, 104
Ostrow, Ronald J., 63
overreaching, 29, 42, 45, 46, 47, 72
oversight as congressional function, 82, 109

partisanship, 45, 47, 80, 81–82, 102
Pastore, John, 30
patronage, 17, 23
Peck, Raymond, 83–89, 179
Perle, Richard, 146, 150, 151
persuasion, 149–52
Pertschuk, Mike, 27, 29, 31, 43, 109; in FTC, 25, 32–35, 36–40
Phillips, Howard, 77, 78
Poindexter, John, 165
political action committees (PACs), 30
Posner, Richard, 23
power, 3, 13, 25, 70
president, 3, 4, 20, 148; attitude toward federal agencies, 5–6, 16, 56; attitude toward managers, 7, 10, 40, 47; reaction to public fears, 45–46; role in federal agencies, 60–61; overruling agencies, 63, 64; concerns of, 70–73, 91, 92; role of in legislative process, 114, 115, 116–17. *See also* loyalty; veto
Presidential Power (Neustadt), xiv
press, 8, 11, 42, 81; appearances and realities in, 48–49
Pressman, Jeffrey, xiv
private groups: power of, 7, 13
process, legislative, 109–12, 139, 164, 166, 176; rules governing, 113–17;

importance of, 127, 129–30; taking
advantage of, 134, 135, 136, 137
rosecutors, federal, 95, 96–97, 103
ublic Integrity Section of Criminal Division, 82
ublic opinion, 7, 25, 45–46, 84, 169;
use of, 47–49
uccio, Tom, 103

uasi-judicial role, 75, 76, 83

ailsback, Thomas F., 134
ayburn, Sam, 167
eagan, Ronald, 9, 46, 52, 84, 88, 149;
EPA and, 7, 44; as governor, 15, 119;
values of, 56, 57–58, 59, 94; attitude
toward federal agencies, 67, 69, 70–
71; LSC and, 76–78, 114; budget issues, 118, 120, 184; MX missile and,
146–47, 152
eality. *See* appearances and reality
eciprocity, 155–56, 171
econciliation, 117–18, 172
egan, Donald, 69, 84
eid, T. R., xiv, 128
esources of influence, 13, 37, 47, 142,
145–46; in MX missile fight, 147–48;
authority and persuasion, 148–51; bargaining, 152; centrality, 153–55; reciprocity and loyalty, 155–56;
configuration of, 156–58; winning,
158–60; increasing, 166–67
esponsibility. *See* common responsibility
among agencies
eynolds, Brad, 69
ichardson, Elliott, 28
ights and interests, 182–83
obinson-Patman Act, 26
oosevelt, Franklin Delano, 185
oosevelt, Theodore, 185
uckelshaus, William, 8–10, 81, 85
ule-making procedures, 35, 37, 41
ules Committee, 116, 149, 168

anderson, James, 44
aturday Night Massacre, 9
awyer, Harold S., 134
chmults, Edward, 68, 69, 70, 73
chwartz, Abba, ix, x
cowcroft Commission, 146, 147, 148

Security and Consular Affairs, Bureau of
(SCA), ix–x, xi
Seidman, Harold, xiv
Senate Commerce Committee, 17, 30
Senate Committee on Labor and Human
Resources, 120, 122, 173–74
Senate Committee on Public Works, 117–
18
Senate Finance Committee, 132
Senate Judiciary Committee, 82, 83
setting for decision-making, 142, 145,
164–65; changing beliefs in, 166–67,
169, 175–77
Shipley, Ruth, ix–x
Smith, Neil, 121, 122, 124
Smith, William French, 56, 57, 58, 59,
61, 69, 70, 73; as attorney general, 65,
68
social security, 178, 185, 187
Social Security Administration, 186
solicitor general, 69, 72–73
Speaker of the House, 113, 141
Stafford, Robert, 174
staffs of federal agencies, 5, 7, 38, 40,
66, 158
stakes, political, 5, 6, 9, 129
State Department, ix, 100, 121
Stockman, David, 9, 76, 180, 182
strategy: defined, 12–15. *See also* common responsibility among agencies;
Federal Trade Commission (FTC); Justice Department; tactics, legislative
Superfund (EPA), 44
support, sources of, 132–33
Supreme Court, 16, 63, 69–70, 71–73,
88–89
Surrey, Stanley, 181

tactics, legislative, 112; concerns of legislators, 125–28; influencing legislators,
128–32; understanding advantages,
134–38; neutralizing opponent's advantages, 139–41; long-run strategy in,
141–44. *See also* House Armed Services Committee; Legal Services Corporation (LSC)
Taking Care of the Law (Bell and Ostrow), 63
tax policy, 156–57
timing, xi, 130, 134, 135, 136, 139

tradition, 7, 8, 57, 67
Treasury Department, 76, 160
Truman, Harry, 46, 185
Tunney, John, 30

unpopular decisions, 74
unresponsiveness, 45, 46

values, 8, 14–15, 67, 75, 95; role of in
  strategy, 62–66
veto, 117, 121, 122, 123, 124; threat of,
  118–19, 170–71
Vietnam, 31, 178
vulnerability, 11, 45–47, 49–53, 93, 95,
  105

Wagner, Robert, 185
Wallace, Larry, 69, 72
"War on Poverty," 29, 119
waste, 45, 46, 50, 52
Watergate, 28, 31, 35, 45, 58; influence
  of, 66, 80, 82, 101, 149
Watt, James, 28
Webster, William, 103
Weicker, Lowell, 121, 122, 123, 164,
  174
Weinberg, Melvin, 101, 102
Weinberger, Caspar W., 15, 25, 43, 81;
  in FTC, 17–18, 20, 21, 36, 42
Williams, Harrison, 101
winning, reputation for, 157, 158–60